translation
Huw Evans
editorial coordination
Giovanna Crespi
editing
Gail Swerling
graphic design
Tassinari/Vetta (CODEsign)
page layout
Chiara Fasoli
cover graphics
CODEsign
technical coordination
Mario Farè
quality control
Giancarlo Berti

Antonio Citterio and Partners
Alessandro Banfi
Clara Buoncristiani, Flos
Ambrogio Busnelli, B&B Italia
Giorgio Busnelli, B&B Italia
Giovanna Calvenzi
Chiara
Antonio Citterio
Marco Conti, Tre più
Natalia Corbetta
Rolf Fehlbaum, Vitra
Gino Finizio
Fiorella
Marillina Fortuna, Arclinea
Francesca
Francesco
Barbara Frey, Visplay
Piero Gandini, Flos
Alessandra Gasparri, Pozzi Ginori
Giovanna
Viviana Giussani
Philippe Grohe, Hansgrohe
Elke Henecka, Vitra
Walter Herbert, Visplay
Bettina Korn, Vitra
Rainer Krause, Anthologie Quartett
Birgit Krück, Ansorg
Claudio Luti, Kartell
Lorena Meroni, Fusital
Ferdinando Mussi, B&B Italia
Toan Nguyen
Alessandra Noto
Enrico Pellegrini
Birgit Pieles, Vitra
Michele Reboli
Daniele Sala, B&B Italia
Ambrogio Spotti, Tisettanta
Studio Fiorella Radice, Tre più
Paolo Tamborrini
Marirosa Toscani Ballo
Fiorella Villa, B&B Italia

Distributed by Phaidon Press
ISBN 1-904313-36-1

www.phaidon.com

© 2004 by Electa, Milan
Elemond Editori Associati
All Rights Reserved

www.electaweb.it

First published in English 2005
© 2005 by Electa Architecture
Mondadori Electa spa, Milan
All Rights Reserved

Printed in Hong Kong

architecture

industrial designer
ANTONIO CITTERIO
alberto bassi

Electaarchitecture

contents

01

antonio citterio industrial designer

A volume on the architect Antonio Citterio's activity as an industrial designer has to reflect several different spheres of interest: first of all it is intended to document a complex and rich career, in quality as well as quantity, that over the course of thirty years has made him one of the greatest of Italian designers, active at the national and international level through his collaboration with numerous important manufacturers.

His figure can serve as the starting point for a wide-ranging reflection on the state of contemporary design, especially in the furnishing sector. This is not only due to the fact that Citterio has played a leading role in the changes that have taken place over the last few decades, but also because he represents a specific example —and one that can in many ways be considered unique—of an architect and designer who has been able to give an original expression and balance to the fundamental elements of the profession. He has taken a synthetic approach to the fields of design, industry, production, research, technology, marketing and consumption that answers to the overall needs of the present day.

The aim of this volume is, on the one hand, to provide tools for a historical analysis of the designer's development, and on the other to embark on a critical examination of his work that will be capable of setting his activity in an appropriate perspective, one that sees it in relation to the changes that have occurred in the culture of design and business and, more generally, in society and individual patterns of behavior.

In the construction of the historical discourse it has proved necessary to assume a phenomenological approach that would take account of a process and the significant stages along its way, by making a series of precise choices with regard to periods of time and selection of the designs. "To be a historian is to carry out a project," Joseph Rykwert has said: "Through the questions that he asks of his material, i.e. the past, the historian has to put together a story. There is no history that is not a story [...] The essential part of a story is selection."[1]

It is hard to fit the figure of Citterio into traditional categories of operation. It is more appropriate to try to bring out the distinctive

[1] "Il progetto della storia," interview with J. Rykwert conducted by V. Magnago Lampugnani, in *Domus*, 683, May 1987.

Quadrante storage unit, Xilitalia-B&B Italia, 1981.

Diesis sofa, B&B Italia, 1979.

Filiberto sofa, Flexform, 1980.

Sity system of sofas, B&B Italia, 1986.

characteristics of his work and give it a precise place in the context of today's design.

Writing about what is contemporary or fairly close to us in time raises obvious questions of method. The conditioning, of which we are conscious to a greater or lesser degree, that stems from daily experience and perception is powerful; the viewpoint of the present has an influence on the investigation and the selection of materials. Renato De Fusco has argued: "We choose to study one event rather than another on the basis of the interest we have in that event today, whether it is recent or remote. This criterion confirms the interpretative character of historiography; it demonstrates that at the root of the historian's work lies the idea of responding to a practical requirement of the present day."[2] Even more evident are the constraints, as well as the opportunities, connected with the fact of focusing attention on a still active figure, within an equally vital entrepreneurial and cultural context, where many of the distinguishing features can be reconstructed on the basis of different types of sources, all of them persuasive.[3]

One of the interesting things about the history of artifacts is that it can form the center of a web of possible accounts, of many different histories connected with all the aspects that shape them and that they in turn generate: economic, productive, technological, marketing and so on.[4] Reference has been made to many of these accounts throughout the book, although without losing sight of the centrality of design as the starting point—and being careful not to take an exclusively expressive and linguistic approach, which would have been of little help in understanding the specific nature of Citterio's contribution.

To respond to these needs, the volume is divided up into a general introduction, followed by three parts covering significant periods of time. Within each of these periods are located descriptive entries on his principal projects of industrial design, mostly in chronological order; some of these, owing to the evident homogeneity of their conceptual and practical approach, are analyzed from a typological perspective and in relation to the manufacturers involved.

On the subject of the architectural project in general, but with an obvious pertinence to industrial design as well, Vittorio Gregotti has recently pointed out that the task of the critic today "is to observe and make clear not only the materials of the project, but also the system of connections with which they are utilized [...] for example the multiplicity of actors involved in the organization of a project [...] not just through

the dialectics with economic, technical and institutional players." And again: "Another of these systems of connection is that of the empirical conditions under which the project operates."[5]

In the case of Citterio's work it has been important to reflect on just this "system of connections" and these "empirical conditions," i.e. on the specific skills involved in the production of commodities and design. In fact the range of factors that guide the designer's work is growing more and more complex. It has become vital to combine the traditional instruments of the discipline with new modes of dialogue with business culture and to give careful consideration to changes in ways of life and living, capable of having a powerful influence on the market.

Citterio has been a good interpreter and mediator of all these innovations: he has united a refined quality of design with a sensitivity—in the broad sense of the word—to cultural and sociological developments (rather than market trends, as it is sometimes rather too simply understood[6]). This has allowed him to grasp the needs of the contemporary world and come up with a correct balance between design, industry and public. This "idea" of the designer—an idea which he has certainly not been the only one to hold, either in the past or the present, but of which he is among the most accredited champions—is also one of the strategies for grappling with the complexities of design, as well as one of the paradigms capable of guiding the expectations and behavior of other designers or companies.

Citterio's activity is very well known, but its quality and value have sometimes encountered difficulties in being recognized by the critics, and even by journalists, especially in Italy.[7] His figure cannot in fact be equated, in the strict sense, with the model of the architect-intellectual: Citterio has for the most part preferred to let others talk about his designs,[8] although he has on occasion made known his position or his thoughts with regard to the activity of teaching.

A certain embarrassment with regard to the architect seems to be linked to a number of misunderstandings. These are connected with the theory and practice of design, and in other ways with the role played by critics, in the specialized or generalist media, especially over the last few years. Recently—although this is a topic which we will only touch on in passing and which deserves further methodological and critical analysis—it has become increasingly common for the easy and iconic product, ideal for the covers of magazines or for the illustrations of coffee-table books, to be presented as "good design." In the

[2] A. D'Auria, R. De Fusco, *Il progetto del design*, Etaslibri, Milan 1992, p. 81.

[3] The compilation of this volume has naturally had to reckon with the specific characteristics of the sources. Alongside the traditional and common bibliographical references, I have turned during the work to the protagonists themselves: the entrepreneurs, designers and collaborators, as well of course as the architect Antonio Citterio, with whom I have had long and fruitful conversations on his work and the themes of his projects.

[4] This is a reflection that can be applied more generally to the methodology of historico-critical research in the sphere of design. For an assessment of the state of the art in historic studies, see E. Castelnuovo, J. Gubler, and D. Matteoni, "L'oggetto misterioso," in *Storia del disegno industriale. 1919–1990. Il dominio del design*, E. Castelnuovo (ed.), vol. III, Electa, Milan 1991; in addition, R. Riccini, "'History from things.' Note sulla storia del disegno industriale," in *Archivi e imprese*, 14, December 1994, pp. 231–35; *Design: storia e storiografia*, Progetto Leonardo, Bologna 1995; A. Bassi, "L'archivio del progetto," in *Archivi e imprese*, 11–12, January–December 1995, pp. 144–60.

[5] V. Gregotti, *Le scarpe di Van Gogh. Modificazioni nell'architettura*, Einaudi, Turin 1994, p. 37.

[6] "New breed of designer-manager who is ultra-sensitive to marketing nuances as well as genuinely expert at his craft" (S. Casciani, *The Art Factory. Italian design: towards the Third Millennium*, Abitare Segesta, Milan 1996, p. 26).

[7] In fact the literature devoted to Citterio is not very extensive. Only two monographs have been published: P. Ciorra, B. Fitoussi and V. Pasca, *Antonio Citterio & Terry Dwan. Architecture & Design 1992–1979*, Artemis, Zurich 1993; P. Ciorra, *Antonio Citterio, Terry Dwan: Ten Years of Architecture and Design*, Birkhäuser, Basel 1995.

[8] This is undoubtedly an attitude shared by many members of the new generation of designers, drawn more to visual communication than to reflection on their own work and its significance. This intellectual limitation, or shift in intellectual tendency, when compared with the stands taken by the generation of the masters of Italian design and the contribution that they made to the cultural debate, can be explained by the altered professional context, but still appears to represent an impoverishment of the debate and the development of the discipline overall.

Metropolis wall container,
Tisettanta, 1984.

Domus fitted wall, B&B Italia,
1989.

assessment of such products due consideration has not been given to the problems of overall approach inherent in industrial design. When Citterio, who practices the profession of industrial designer seriously in terms of substance, quantity and method, brings his objects onto the market, there are many who criticize his production, concluding that there is nothing innovative about it and underlining its middle-of-the-road character. They disapprove of his avowed sources of inspiration and observe that while Citterio's products sell in large numbers and are methodologically correct, they are not always self-referential from the viewpoint of their image.

The architect himself has argued that "design should not be confused with its photographic representation, with its capacity [...] to present an image," and that it is necessary instead to "move from what might be called ideological design, which aims to affirm a tendency, to a real product that people will buy and use."[9] These statements are clearly connected with the understanding of industrial design. Without getting into the endless dispute over its defini-

tion, it seems possible to say that part of the confusion stems from the altered and uncertain disciplinary and terminological status (especially today and specifically in the sector of furniture) of the word itself, which is used by many people in completely different ways: everything has turned into design, nothing is design any longer. The presumed democratization of the term, and of information about the field and its communication, has cloaked everything in an aura of uncertainty where the different is the same, and it is no longer possible to recognize either its specific character or its merit.[10]

Essentially Citterio's activity in the field of industrial design has shifted the focus of theoretical and practical debate, prefiguring a pragmatic approach that concentrates totally on problem-solving. The direction he has taken is certainly not the only appropriate way of tackling the design of the artifacts of *surmodernité* (to use Marc Augé's expression[11]), but he does appear to have grasped some of its characteristics. Otherwise it would be hard to explain Citterio's popularity with the major manufacturers, the success of his

[9] "Minimalismo come complessità. Intervista con Antonio Citterio," interview conducted by V. Pasca in *Interni*, "Annual casa," 1994, pp. 26–33. He has also said: "On the one hand there are industrial products, on the other those linked to a need for expression. Often it is the latter that critics tend to recognize" (conversation with the author, Milan, July 8, 2003).
[10] In this connection see also the illuminating M. Perniola, *Contro la comunicazione*, Einaudi, Turin 2004.
[11] There is an extensive literature on the philosophical and terminological aspects of the postindustrial phase, to which we refer the reader. With respect to the uncritical interpretations and practices of the "magnificent and progressive destiny" of the postmodern globalized system, some recent analyses from different perspectives are certainly stimulating: to take just two examples, those of Zygmunt Bauman and Marc Augé.

AC office chairs, Vitra, 1990.

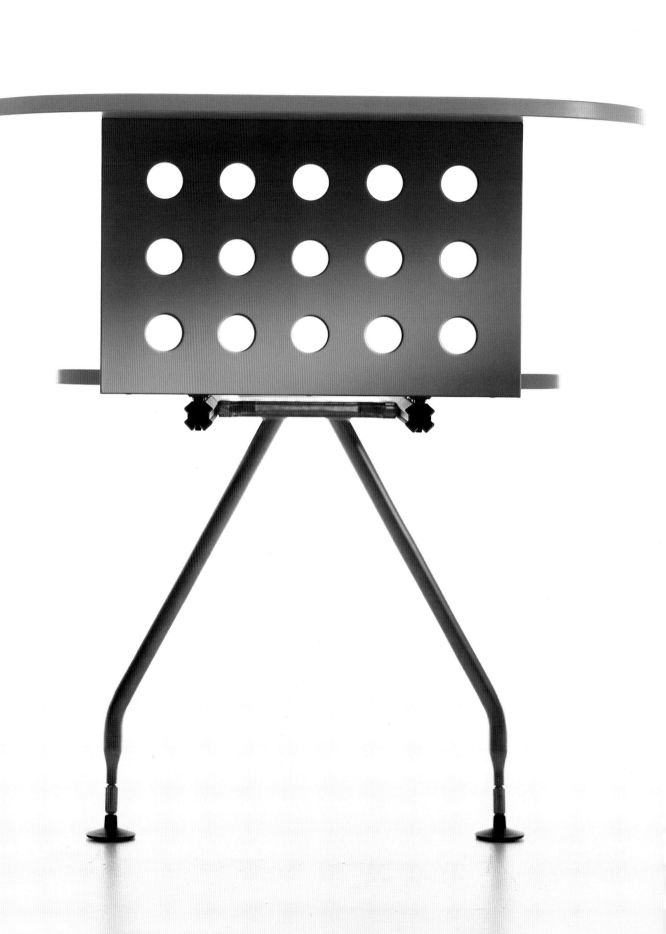

products and the esteem in which he is held by his colleagues: he is not "the" model, but "one" credible model that we need to try to understand.

The tradition of Italian design and the new condition of contemporary artifacts

Citterio is an architect by training, methodology and the nature of his approach to design, applied on different scales of intervention, from architecture to interiors (private, public or service) and from the design of temporary or permanent exhibits to industrial design, whether that of the single product, a system or an overall strategy. The fact that he was born in Meda, in Brianza,[12] at the heart of one of the key areas of the Italian system of furnishing and design, is important. He received a significant part of his training "on the job," in close contact with the world of handicrafts or mechanized craftwork. This was then rapidly transformed into an up-to-date model of advanced industrialization, eventually developing into the contemporary mode of operation in the complex system of economic and cultural globalization, and of the delocalization of production.[13]

During the over thirty years of the architect's activity, it is possible to distinguish at least three fundamental periods, marked by significant shifts in the professional opportunities open to him, by the renewal or widening of the group of his collaborators and by the transfer of his studio, which has entailed making structural and operational changes.

The period of his training and his early, already successful experiences in the seventies (culminating in the Diesis sofa and Quadrante bookcase) was followed by the watershed of the mid-eighties, when he established his reputation in the field of design (with the Sity range of sofas in particular), embarked on numerous collaborations with important companies and received his first architectural commissions. This process of continual growth, straddling two millennia, reached its climax with the opening of a new studio in the center of Milan, providing him with an up-to-date operations base to meet the growing demand for his professional services.

Over the span of this long career it is possible to trace several constant areas of intervention: first,

[12] See the extensive literature on the manufacturing region of Brianza and the Italian model in general, commencing with the useful summary by U. Colombo, "Caratteri peculiari del modello produttivo industriale italiano," in *Il modello italiano. Le forme della creatività*, O. Calabrese (ed.), Skira, Milan 1998, pp. 3–13.
[13] On what is happening in the economic, industrial and commercial system, from the perspective of design, see, among others, A. Branzi, *Il Design italiano 1964–1990*, Electa, Milan 1996; *Grafica e design a Milano 1933–2000*, A. Colonetti (ed.), Abitare Segesta, Milan 2001; *La cultura dell'abitare. Il design in Italia 1945–2001*, G. Bosoni (ed.), Skira, Milan 2002; *Il modello italiano. Le forme della creatività*, O. Calabrese (ed.), Skira, Milan 1998; *Design 2000*, E. Mucci (ed.), Franco Angeli, Milan 1994; and more specifically, for example, G. Lojacono, *Le imprese del sistema arredamento. Strategie di design, prodotto e distribuzione*, ETAS, Milan 2001.

Ad Hoc office desk, Vitra, 1994.

Visavis office chairs, Vitra, 1992.

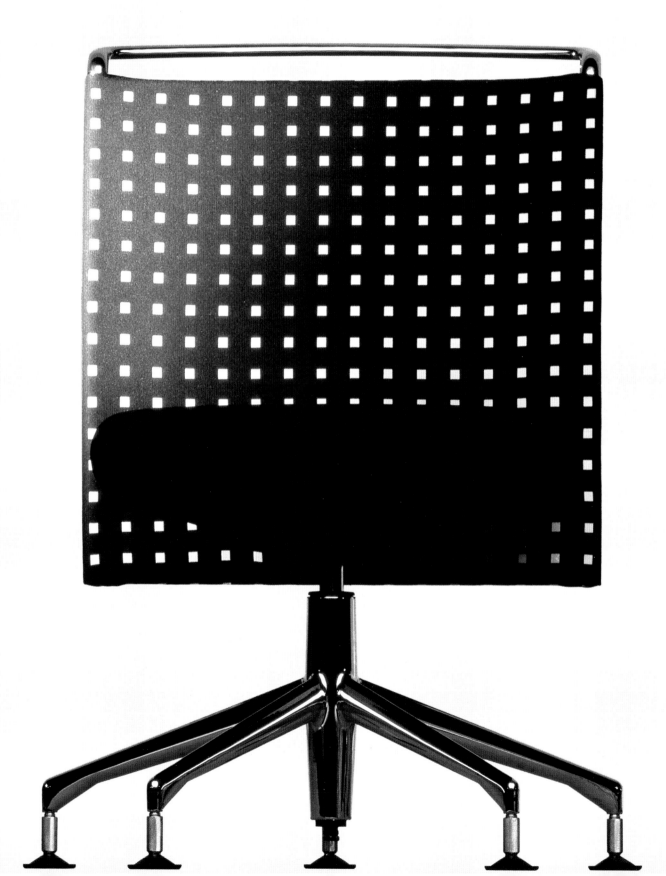

the domestic environment, in all its typological and spatial inflections (kitchen, bathroom, living space, etc.), and then the office and lighting, not forgetting exhibit design for commercial as well as noncommercial purposes. Over time his focus has shifted in the direction of a systemic approach to product design, with an all-embracing intervention of management and control.[14]

Italian industrial design
On the one hand Citterio's work is in line with the tradition and characteristics of Italian design, and on the other it presents aspects of discontinuity.
At the base of the cultural and commercial success of industrial design in Italy it is possible to identify several distinctive elements, especially during the initial phase in the fifties and sixties, which was in turn rooted in the theoretical and methodological choices of the years between the wars. Vittorio Gregotti has summed up the specific characteristics of that period: "The relatively small size of companies and the possibilities of flexibility and experimentation connected with it; the ability and aggressiveness of the new

entrepreneur, and at times his sincere attraction to the world of culture; the presence of a skilled and not very fragmented workforce, wedded to its craft roots and therefore capable of making a creative contribution, and of seeing the product as a whole; lastly a group of designers (almost all of them architects in the Italian case) of great ability and talent that often went unexpressed in the architectural sector but were brought into play at the special moment of the foundation of the specific profession of industrial designer [...]. Finally a society, and thus a public of consumers as well, in a phase of rapid and radical transformation toward a new sense of the relationship between consumption and accumulation." And on the specific question of furniture, Gregotti declares: "Italian design in the sector of the home was certainly, in those years, more ready to try out new materials, to propose new technologies of production and to let itself be affected by influences that came directly from experiences in industry and in the visual arts."[15]
Decisive too was the concept of *deroga* or "departure from the rules," as Renzo Zorzi has

[14] "He seems to us to be one of the Italian designers who has been most successful in taking the project from the exhaustive dimension of the individual object to the open and dynamic one of the coordinated system" (E. Morteo, "Antonio Citterio," in *Un'industria per il design. La ricerca, i designers, l'immagine B&B Italia*, M. Mastropietro and R. Gorla (eds.), Lybra Image, Milan 1999, p. 264). A succinct introduction to these themes is provided by the analysis conducted by V. Pasca in P. Ciorra, B. Fitoussi and V. Pasca, *Antonio Citterio & Terry Dwan. Architecture & Design 1992–1979*, cit., pp. 19–27.
[15] V. Gregotti, "Premessa," in *Un'industria per il design. La ricerca, i designers, B&B Italia*, cit., p. 22. Interesting in this connection, among others, C. Demattè, "I segreti del sistema dell'offerta. L'innovazione nelle aziende piccole e medie dei settori per la casa," in *La cultura dell'abitare. Il design in Italia 1945–2001*, cit., pp. 62–73.

AC2 office chair, Vitra, 1990.

Mobile Elements system of office furniture, Vitra, 2002.

Camera spotlight,
Ansorg, 1996.

defined it, made possible by an "extraordinarily lively, relentless and obsessive entrepreneurship, determined to clear itself a way out of the world of handicrafts." A way that made it possible to "emerge from that early, more restrictive, definition of method in industrial production, insisting more on the values of design, the study of materials and their specific technologies, the significance of the object's form (and image), its suitability to the use to which it is put, its adaptability to the setting and the range of intentions, of culture, with which the designer loads it, or from which he liberates it, rather than on the preeminent value of mass production."[16] In essence, according to Sergio Polano's analysis, the finest products of Italian design appear to be "characterized by an attempt at an original synthesis of experimental subversion and rationality."[17]

With respect to this tradition, the second part of the seventies and eighties—in relation to the position of Italian design in the international context as well—represented a moment of clear change from the viewpoints of the industrial organization of production, distribution and marketing, of the role of the designer (as well as research into the language of design) and of the mechanisms of culture and consumption in general. Without any pretense to exhausting the subject, which strictly speaking pertains to other levels of inquiry and argument, it seems opportune here to single out some of the elements that contributed to this change.

Fashion, minimalism, contemporary design
One aspect that needs to be considered—and which is only in appearance secondary—is the recognition and success of Italian fashion,[18] and the implicit and explicit effect that this has had on design. Not without contradictions, one part of the culture of design has been influenced by fashion design and has adopted some of its methods, not just with regard to the act of design itself, but also and above all in relation to questions of identity, image and communication.[19]
Vanni Pasca has written: "A series of designers, especially designers of furniture, have looked to fashion stylists with the idea that in design too it would be possible to bring a new type of designer into the foreground with respect to the industries, a creative figure characterized not so much by his research or method as by a clearly recognizable image in the media."[20] In addition, the model of the fashion system—in its aspects of the organization of production, the logics of distribution and marketing and even the banal

question of timing the renewal of the product—has undeniably had an influence on the strategic and operational choices made by the design system as a whole, as well as providing a "benchmark," at once real and cultural in the broad sense, for manufacturers and designers.[21] The nineties were to be characterized by so-called minimalism. The designation is a highly ambiguous one.[22] It is based on references to the world of artistic research and implies an ethical and ascetic tendency largely foreign to the majority of designers and products to which this label is attached. It would be more appropriate to see it, as Fulvio Carmagnola does, as "a common movement of reduction: of the form, the values, the resources. That design should have reacted to this unsettling cultural circumstance with a return to simplicity seems to be, as it were, the internal repercussion of an overall perception of reduction, of impoverishment, through the filter of the specific sensibility of design: a filter that once again places the emphasis on the need for rigor, for abstraction, in what almost amounts to a sense of guilt with regard to the excesses of decoration in the recent past."[23]
For Pasca "minimalism constitutes the taking to extremes of a culture of design that favors simplicity over formal agitation, the reduction of signs over superfluity, laconism over confused representation, reserve over effusion."[24] And he points out that Italian design (and this is certainly a consideration that can be extended to Citterio's work) "has always practiced a temperate rationalism, attentive to tradition and to the typology of furnishings."[25] It appears, in short, that this minimalist trend can be traced back to a neo-rationalist current that is reasserting itself within a general tendency to a "new simplicity."
The pair of factors introduced—the comparison with the fashion system and the wholesale adoption of the language of minimalism—are evidently related to the transformation that has taken place in the organization of industry and production, in the ownership, financial, commercial and distributive structure of the sector of furniture design.
Manolo De Giorgi provides a useful clarification of the context of operation that has determined an essentially new relationship between designer and manufacturer when he argues that "industries without designers" have been created. By this he means "not so much the disappearance of the designer, as the fact that he has been overshadowed by corporate culture to the point where this itself has become the scheme and destiny of design [...]. It is the brand that leads the dance of design, it is to the brand that

[16] R. Zorzi, "Introduzione," in *Un'industria per il design. La ricerca, i designers, l'immagine B&B Italia*, cit., p. 28.
[17] S. Polano, *Achille Castiglioni, tutte le opere 1938–2000*, Electa, Milan 2001, p. 9.
[18] See the literature on Italian fashion, but also the thoughtful U. Volli, *Contro la moda*, Feltrinelli, Milan 1988.
[19] See, among others, *1951–2001 Made in Italy?*, L. Settembrini (ed.), Skira, Milan 2001.
[20] V. Pasca, "Il design italiano: elementi per una storia," in *1951–2001 Made in Italy?*, cit., p. 109.
[21] To take just one example, relating to the process of creation of the product, Giannino Malossi has pointed out that "the discovery of differentiation as an economic and marketing resource that determines the design of products today [...] has borrowed from fashion a vocabulary of expression that does not spurn decoration, color or the clothing of the 'body' [...] of objects" (G. Malossi, "Design di moda?" in *ADI Design Index 1998-1999*, Editrice Compositori, Bologna 2000, p. 35). These methods were not extraneous to the research and practice of design (on these questions see for example A. Branzi, *The Hothouse. Italian New Wave Design*, Thames & Hudson, London 1984; E. Manzini, *Artefatti. Verso una nuova ecologia dell'ambiente artificiale*, Domus Academy, Milan 1990; *Le superfici del design*, M. Barberis (ed.), Idea Books-Progetto DIR, Milan 1991), which however has partly shifted its attention in just this direction, reinterpreting some requirements of the contemporary market in the light of this comparison and these stimuli.
[22] Minimalism has been defined as a portmanteau word, "a term that [...] has over time brought about, in at first an erratic and haphazard way and then with increasing intensity, a sort of slippage with respect to its original domain, an extension of its semantic aura into much broader areas, to the point of becoming, in certain cases, the dominant trait of a culture" (F. Carmagnola, "La conoscenza della conoscenza," in F. Carmagnola and V. Pasca, *Minimalismo etica delle forme e nuova semplicità del design*, Lupetti, Milan 1996, p. 9).
[23] *Ibid.*, p. 13. All this "seems to be a substitute for elegant epicurean poverty, child of the fatigue with excess. And the quest for gaps and differences in the very fabric of fullness, in order to find, through images, the balance of things" (*ibid.*, p. 29).
[24] V. Pasca, "Design degli anni novanta. Minimalismo e neorazionalismo," in F. Carmagnola and V. Pasca, *Minimalismo etica delle forme e nuova semplicità del design*, cit., p. 63.
[25] *Ibid.*, p. 109.

everything can be traced back." In this way, he continues, the central role appears to have been taken by "corporate culture and the policy of the brand as a means of finding a way through the semantic fog produced by the myriad products of turn-of-the-century culture."[26]

On the one hand, therefore, we have a relatively homogenizing, recognizable and reassuring language of design like minimalism, which sees the attention to the (real or presumed) demands of the consumer as a priority, achieving in essence a different point of equilibrium between the elements that go into constructing the approach to design. On the other stands the "fashionable" choice of focusing decisively on promotion of the brand, sometimes at the expense of another way of understanding product research that is historically part of the genes and genius of Italian design and that was born, in a fairly spontaneous manner, with the aspiration to be definitive, timeless, to become a classic. So this appears to be the difference from the contemporary option, which does not fail, instead, to yield to the tempta-

tion of the double label: corporate brand plus "name" of the designer.

To put it in a nutshell, two predominant modes of design-driven action seem to have become established, from the strategic and linguistic viewpoint: companies that, as Pasca again argues, "aim to design series characterized by the reference to a formally homogeneous domestic setting, into which each piece of furniture fits because it contributes to the definition of a coherent trend in taste [...] or on the contrary companies that set out to produce individual pieces, independent of one another, characterized only by a number of constants of form, material or technology, which serve to define the manufacturer's image."[27]

On the one hand these options tally with the historic activity of companies and designers (such as, to take one paradigmatic example, Vico Magistretti's work for De Padova). On the other, they have opened up new directions that have been followed by young designers, along different roads and in different ways. It is sufficient to compare the approach of Michele De Lucchi,

[26] M. De Giorgi, "Premessa alla nuova edizione," in *Un'industria per il design. La ricerca, i designers, l'immagine B&B Italia*, cit., p. 17.
[27] V. Pasca, "Il design italiano: elementi per una storia," in *1951–2001 Made in Italy?*, cit., p. 113.

Battista trolley-table, Kartell, 1991.

Spoon stool, Kartell, 2003.

Dolly chair, Kartell, 1996.

Mobil storage units, Kartell, 1994.

ABC armchair, Flexform, 1998.

Freetime sofa, B&B Italia, 1999.

Marcel sofa, B&B Italia, 2003.

inspirer and interpreter of the culture of enterprises like Olivetti, the Italian Post Office or ENEL, with the "global" intervention of Citterio himself, and then of an entire generation of designers, from Rodolfo Dordoni to Piero Lissoni, or again (taking a "joint" workshop approach) Alessandro Mendini's work with Alessi or Swatch.[28]

Contemporary artifacts and new patterns of consumption
Some aspects given only cursory consideration so far constitute inescapable elements of the context. And then further reflection needs to be given to the present-day condition of artifacts,[29] a question that has been illuminated by the contributions of sociologists, anthropologists and philosophers.
The contemporary era has seen the definitive establishment of a system based on the "symbolic economy":[30] "an aesthetics corresponding to the impure or functional symbolic economy," in Carmagnola's words, "that no longer recognizes its root in the classic coupling of use value/exchange value." Fashion and design have become the key locations of aestheticization and of the contaminated system of cultural merchandise. On the other hand the new condition of objects is related to a different trend in consumption.
For Giovanni Siri "the consumer follows the logic of desires and not of need, of impulse and not of necessity, of aesthetics and not of ethics, of play and not of rationality,"[31] and thus passes from a system of needs to one of wants. Need and desire have different logics; desires are deferrable, stimulated by the mechanisms of emotion, not so much and not just by necessities.
This is the context of the activity of design and production, characterized—for Giampaolo Fabris—by the "capacity to grasp changes in the consumer's tastes immediately, sensitivity in meeting the needs of the market as well as possible, a particular attention to the aesthetic component [...], types of innovation that our country has shown it is able to handle at a level of excellence."[32]
So industry and designer have been working for some time on a "new artifact," one that is no longer just a question of form/function,[33] but endowed with other "qualities." An artifact that fits into an overall strategy (of which the designer is frequently the author and/or the co-star) of distribution, display in sales outlets and communication.
At this point, for Andrea Branzi, design "as a permanent avant-garde workshop is collaborating

from the outside in an uninterrupted revision of the range of merchandise and the models of development of the postindustrial system, and assuming on the inside a strategic role in the evaluation of the structures created, stimulating evolutionary developments in entire sectors of production."[34]
On the one hand what is being realized, in unexpected ways, is the utopia of modernity, intent on a total involvement of design in the industrial process, on the "unity of the arts"; on the other this has been to a great extent emptied of the lofty and other aims that used to underpin it. To quote Branzi again: "Designing without questions, and therefore without answers. A design without metaphysics and therefore without tragedy, and so present, active, but with no definable destiny [...]. A design that produces information and services, develops new links and filters new relationships, but that no longer describes a unified scenario, and does not provide the complexity of the system with islands of meaning. A design that is part of a weak, slow, realistic reformism."[35]

"The designer is the man who runs the risk of his idea"
The set of elements discussed so far represents one part of the panorama in which the activity of the architect Citterio is located, acts and finds a specific significance and key of interpretation.
His method of working has made use of an original form of dialogue and comparison with a number of different methodological and linguistic approaches pertaining to the traditional culture of design.
A first reference derives from the sphere of Italian proto-rationalist and rationalist architecture between the wars, and in particular the schools of Como and Milan. His training, which did not consist solely of a university education, was very personal and conducted independently of indications, stimuli and transitory tendencies that came from "outside." Rather it was inspired by an inner quest and a comparison by "elective affinities" with the masters, following a course aimed at the identification of strong orientations in design. It is these which have permitted him to pass through profoundly different moments in history, spurred on chiefly by a personal continuity and consistency.
It is easy to discern the effect of the rationalist lesson on Citterio's architecture, from Casa Busnelli to his most recent works. But this model, seen in terms of essentiality, cleanliness of design and form and care taken over the use of materials and the handling of details, has also

[28] It would be worth taking a look at the role of the "workshops" that have developed over the years around charismatic figures like Alessandro Mendini, and above all Ettore Sottsass Jr. In this connection and only in passing, it is useful to recall the difficulties encountered by the great masters of design in creating, beyond and sometimes even through university teaching, a "school" of designers: Zanuso, Castiglioni, Mari and Magistretti have not designated their own "heirs." A failure to leave a legacy, for whatever reason, that seems to have had repercussions on the new generations of designers, especially in Italy, and perhaps even on the contemporary identity of the manufacturers.
[29] Several authors have described the context of the end of the grand narratives, of ideologies, of all-embracing bodies of knowledge that, excluding "on principle the acceptance of a metaphysical discourse," "highlighted the pragmatic function of knowledge" (M. Vitta, *Il progetto della bellezza. Il design fra arte e tecnica, 1851–2001*, Einaudi, Turin 2001, p. 310). From this derives, according to Gregotti, the loss of the "critical" role of design (V. Gregotti, *Le scarpe di Van Gogh. Modificazioni nell'architettura*, cit., p. 19).
[30] "It is clear that the symbolic economy, polarized around specific goods like the products of design and fashion, is closely complementary and not opposed to the processes of abstract and immaterial exploitation of the new economy" (F. Carmagnola, *Vezzi insulsi e frammenti di storia universale. Tendenze estetiche nell'economia del simbolico*, Luca Sossella, Rome 2001, p. 29).
[31] G. Siri, *La psiche del consumo*, Franco Angeli, Milan 2001, also cited in G. Fabris, *Il nuovo consumatore: verso il postmoderno*, Franco Angeli, Milan 2003, p. 49. On these themes, and on the concept of merchandise-knowledge, see G. Maione, *Le merci intelligenti. Miti e realtà del capitalismo contemporaneo*, Bruno Mondadori, Milan 2001.
[32] G. Fabris, *Il nuovo consumatore: verso il postmoderno*, cit., p. 237.
[33] We will not go here into the question of the other spirits of Italian design, culturally and ideologically revived by, among others, Branzi's interpretation in the key of "Neodesign." See too G. De Michelis, *Aperto, molteplice, continuo*, Dunod, Milan 1998.
[34] A. Branzi, *Introduzione al design italiano. Una modernità incompleta*, Baldini&Castoldi, Milan 1999, p. 170.
[35] *Ibid.*, p. 175.

had a clear influence on his interior and industrial design, which is the focus of our interest here.

This has resulted in a continual exchange between the two poles: on the one hand the one-off piece or the self-referential and self-sufficient system, on the other the tendency and the necessity to consider the overall relation of the object designed to the space in which it is set. "Architecture is born in a specific place, on a site, as if it had roots," declares Citterio.[36] Of course this is not true for industrial design, yet it does not seem accidental that part of his recent research has been aimed essentially at binding products and systems to predetermined organizations of space. This is a response to the need to provide almost standardized keys in order to meet the needs of production based on an "industrial" logic. They are works oriented toward a global approach to the design of interiors, of single types of room, which prefigures a programmatically integral solution to each specific requirement of furnishing: from the kitchen to the bathroom, from the living area to the office, in a sort of industrial interior design that ranges from product design to the design of the individual piece or system and then all the way to the comprehensive design of spaces.

Citterio's interest in models from the United States and the work of Charles and Ray Eames in particular has been fundamental. The two American designers were significant for the lessons contained in their products and for the indications that they provided about the designer's role in relation to industry. Their attitude was characterized by a marked pragmatism, by a search for agreement and by an identification with the needs of the manufacturer, and yet was backed up by a propensity for innovation, in the use of materials and in technical and functional solutions, and by an attention to purpose and modes of use. What fascinated him about the Eames was the overall balance of their design and the care lavished on details of execution and production. On the tradition of American design in general, Maurizio Vitta has written: "The role of design seems to be incorporated into a meticulously formulated company strategy […], it expressed a devotedly utilitarian character

[36] Conversation with the author, Milan, June 27, 2003.

Emme hospital bed, Industrie Guido Malvestio, 1992.

rather than one of image." And he continues: "the relationship between art and technique [...] is tackled [...] in terms of efficiency, method, empiricism."[37] In the work of the masters of American design—sticking to furniture, from George Nelson to Florence Knoll—the central question of the project has always been the correct relationship between product and user, seen as creation of the best possible conditions for a product to be first understood, then bought and correctly utilized, and finally to have characteristics of physical and aesthetic durability in time.

Design, Citterio has argued, is a "value intrinsic to the product. Design means planning and planning signifies dealing with industrial reality [...]. It does not mean bowing to the arid rules of marketing, but accepting reality and making it tangible in order to think about what does not yet exist, to think about invention, or simply and this is not easy—to improve what already exists."[38]

And again: "Products are interesting when they appear fully resolved, otherwise one cannot speak of research."[39] Significant in this connection is the concept of "continuous design" that underpins a substantial part of the architect's work: operating on the product and the market not with an obsession to come up with something new at any cost, and at a rapid pace, but making an incessant effort of fine-tuning, of refinement of solutions, starting out from an initial intuition that is tested through constant revision. Citterio again: "The market is an inescapable parameter of design [...]. The constraints imposed by marketing, production, materials and logistics do not represent an obstacle for me. Instead I regard them as a challenge in which creativity and inventiveness play a key role in the definition of the product."[40]

This mode of operation seems to be inspired by what sociologists have defined fine-tuning:[41] an increasingly refined adaptation of the product to meet the needs of production and design, as well as the market. Taking this approach, Citterio has focused on grand typological themes, methods of tackling problems that take a long view, ideas sensed and perfected through improvements and refinements. It is not hard to identify, for instance, a number

[37] M. Vitta, *Il progetto della bellezza. Il design fra arte e tecnica, 1851–2001*, cit., p. 295.
[38] G. Finizio, "La riduzione del segno," in *Ottagono*, September–October 1994, p. 83.
[39] Conversation with the author, Milan, July 8, 2003.
[40] G. Finizio, "La riduzione del segno," cit., p. 84. "There have been times," declares Citterio, "when it was easier to be 'creative'; the conditions were different. The problem is that you can't afford to make mistakes today, among other things because large investments in machinery, technology and human resources are involved" (conversation with the author, Milan, July 18, 2003).
[41] G. Fabris, *Il nuovo consumatore: verso il postmoderno*, cit., p. 105.

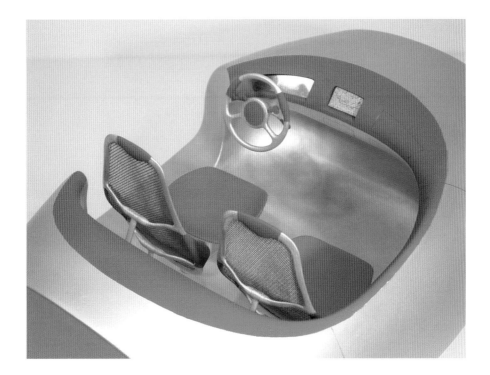

Concept of interiors for an "advanced sports car," Alfa Romeo, 2000.

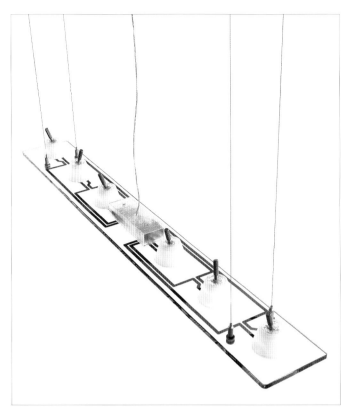

of constants in his design of padded furniture, from the idea of the island (born with the Sity, and still present in the recent Charles and Marcel) to the supported-supporting relationship, i.e. the construction of a structure on which rests a covering or padding, an idea that is essentially of architectural origin; or again the sofa as a product of "tailoring," a structure to be suitably dressed through the cut of the fabric.

Equally evident in the case of seating is the theme of the reappraisal and redesign of classical or archetypal forms, drawn from the tradition of the anonymous craftsman or that of industrial design. Following this line, Citterio has on the one hand introduced largely functional variations, and on the other taken up the challenge issued by technological systems and materials. "Technological processes," he argues, "represent the new threshold of design, whether they concern a material, an innovative textile or the confrontation with advanced electronic interfaces."[42] What characterizes his activity as a designer overall, according to Enrico Morteo, is the "reinterpretation of a number of constants of bourgeois furnishing" and the shifting on the "horizon of design, beyond the canonical goals of functionalism, in search of symbolic values capable of satisfying the demands of a now fully affluent society."[43]

Citterio's designs, whether they are for single objects, for coordinated systems, or answer to the new logic of the approach taken by industrial design to spaces, are intended for a market that has overcome technical and functional constraints and regional or national cultural restrictions. They are global products that nevertheless communicate a local origin, declaring their provenance (although sometimes no longer the place of their production in the strict sense), their pertinence to a culture of business and design. They aspire to an ideal, transnational user, and yet are capable of conveying the characteristics and qualities of the "Italian way" of design, even when these are attained by working with international companies.[44]

On the subject of the link between designer and manufacturer, Citterio has stressed the decisive role played by the client on several occasions.

[42] Conversation with the author, Milan, July 8, 2003.
[43] E. Morteo, "Antonio Citterio," in *Un'industria per il design. La ricerca, i designers, l'immagine B&B Italia*, cit., pp. 259-60.
[44] More generally speaking, this is a condition common to contemporary products, but which had not always been true of Italian design, frequently distinguished by a style and connotations that could be defined in various ways as "local," endowed with marked elements of identity, on which their success was in the end based. The attainment of a balance between a global system, culture and language and the identity of local characteristics certainly represents a challenge and an opportunity for the future of the industries of design in our country.

Lastra hanging lamp, Flos, 1998.

Kelvin table lamp, Flos, 2003.

Concept for a television set, Brionvega, 1999.

[45] Conversation with the author, Milan, July 8, 2003.
[46] L. Asnaghi, "Citterio, o la semplicità come etica," insert in *Affari e finanza*, November 6, 2000.
[47] This concept has recently led to talk of "highly sophisticated mannerism," in S. Casciani, "Costruire ad Amburgo," in *Domus*, November 2002, pp. 74–87.
[48] G. Finizio, "La riduzione del segno," cit., p. 83.
[49] C. Morozzi, "Ritratto di un designer: in viaggio alla ricerca dei maestri," in *Modo*, 85, November 1985, p. 33.

A collaboration is effective if it is based on a personal and direct rapport with the decision-making centers (be they proprietors, administrators or directors of research and development centers), and thus capable of rendering the entire process fruitful and essential: "Design has a father and a mother, a designer and a manufacturer who work together to produce a result; a good product is frequently associated with a good client."[45] In a phase of fragmentation of decision-making roles and areas of competence (sometimes to the point of confusion), which has undeniably characterized some recent developments in the organization of contemporary companies, these are certainly significant experiences that hark back to the "strong" ties between entrepreneur and architect typical of Italian design in the past. "More with less" is one of the ideas that inspire his approach to design: "Everything I do is simple," he has said. "Careful though: the simplest thing is the hardest to produce. I realize that I have reached my goal with a project when I cannot find anything else to take away because I have got down to the essence."[46]

This way of tackling design implies an empirical, realistic attitude, coupled with extreme care, from the overall conception down to the handling of details, aimed at an end result of balanced "smoothness."[47]
This realism has been seen by some as aridity or mediocrity of inspiration. But Citterio claims: "Being realistic does not mean lacking 'poetry.'"[48] The question of Citterio's poetics is moreover an old one, if as far back as 1985 an attentive observer like Cristina Morozzi could argue in *Modo*: "Making poetry signifies leaving a mark, being constructive: this is what interests him, not demonstrating continuity, or a continual capacity for diversification."[49] Another aspect of Citterio's work that the author of the article singled out was the "facility" that characterized his approach to design and the products themselves, a *lievitas* he shares with other prolific furniture designers, commencing with Vico Magistretti. This is a significant quantitative dimension, built up over the relatively short space of thirty years, and one that has to be tackled in any historic and critical analysis. Another question

Eileen table, B&B Italia, 2003.

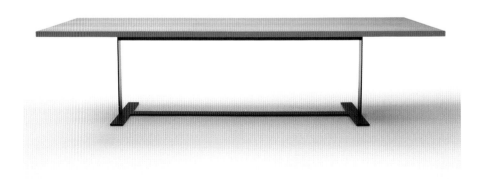

raised by Citterio's work concerns what Zorzi has defined as "departure from the rules," the ability to deviate, to introduce innovation, in the broad sense, into the product.[50]

Anyone who meets Citterio gets the impression that he has a thorough grasp of the profession; sometimes one might expect more from him, whatever this may mean: in some ways the architect appears more in tune with the "problems" of industry and/or the consumer than with his own expressive needs. "I'm interested in projects," he says in fact, "where there is a problem to be solved: technical, functional, typological, aesthetic."[51] He has practically never designed decorative objects, such as pieces of pottery or blown glass.

Thus the doubt arises that the "departure" in Citterio's design is a wholly "internal" one: within the construction of the overall project in the first place, then within the products, in the elaborate search for correct solutions—for industry and user—to problems, and again in the carefully worked-out details of his objects.[52] "In my work there is a certain discontinuity in the language," he says, "but an extreme recognizability in the method adopted."[53] This approach seems to be aimed at constructing a sort of complex naturalness, an apparently effortless outcome but one that is in reality the result of an elaborate process.[54]

In the investigation and analysis of Citterio's activity as an industrial designer there is one statement of his that appears particularly apt, helping us to grasp the underlying sense of his work, and more in general the possible condition of design in the present and the near future: "The designer is the man who runs the risk of his idea. He is the one who gets close to the heart of the company and interprets its potentialities."[55]

Vilém Flusser has written: "The term design has succeeded in carving itself out a key position in everyday language because we are beginning (perhaps rightly) no longer to believe that art and technique are sources of value, and to become aware of the intention (design) that sustains them." Because in essence "the concept of design is replacing that of idea."[56]

[50] Enzo Mari argues: "The quality of a design depends on the degree, however minimal, of cultural change that it triggers" (E. Mari, *Progetto e passione*, Bollati Boringhieri, Turin 2001, p. 52).
[51] "I find it hard to do projects where there is no problem; I'm interested in working when something has to be solved, not just out of a need for expression. In architecture, for example, there is always a problem" (conversation with the author, Milan, December 10, 2003).
[52] Citterio has declared: "I don't like the detail for its own sake, the detail as the dominant element, which overshadows the rest" ("Il progetto della qualità. Colloquio con Antonio Citterio," interview conducted by V. Pini, in *Interni*, "Annual casa," 1992, p. 58).
[53] Conversation with the author, Milan, February 23, 2004.
[54] "I am interested in the normality of objects; I seek the result in naturalness, a complex naturalness" (conversation with the author, Milan, July 8, 2003).
[55] G. Finizio, "La riduzione del segno," cit., p. 84.
[56] V. Flusser, *The Shape of Things: A Philosophy of Design*, Reaktion, London 1999.

Mart armchairs, B&B Italia, 2003.

02

1968–85. in the system of italian design

The period of time stretching from the end of the sixties to the middle of the eighties covers Citterio's training and his initial experiences in the field of design. The methods and characteristics that distinguished this early phase were to have a great influence on his subsequent orientation and choices. Decisive in the first place was the fact that he was born in Meda, in the heart of what was emerging as the furniture manufacturing region of Brianza: a situation characterized by the presence of a large number of cottage industries (whose origin can be traced back to the agricultural character of the area), which began to industrialize immediately after the war, with each company taking a different road.

There can be no doubt that one of the factors which favored this development was the contribution of architects—from Gio Ponti to Marco Zanuso—who were asked to collaborate with the manufacturers by entrepreneurs who were as enlightened as they were practical. Some of these companies were able to grow by building on a solid experience of craftsmanship, as happened with Cassina for example; others, like Arflex or C&B, set up in a fertile context of production that was able to draw on a series of useful "environmental" prerequisites, invested from the outset in new materials and technologies.

The second half of the sixties brought another turning point as the manufacturers of the Brianza region made decisive moves in the direction of a new organization of production and a close collaboration between company and designer. By now this approach had superseded the traditional production of period furniture both numerically and culturally. Citterio frequented the art college in Cantù, where he took his school-leaving examinations: his teachers included Giuliano Vangi and Annarosa Bernasconi, instructors in life drawing and architectural drawing respectively, and Professor Busnelli, an artist whose lessons Citterio attended during the summer months. Also connected with the circles of the art college (where Citterio would return to teach in 1971–72) were the architects Albizzoni, Genghini and Valtorta, in whose studio he went to work at the age of seventeen. Rolando Gorla, Vittorio Prato and Federico Busnelli, whom Citterio was to meet at

Antonio Citterio and
Paolo Nava's studio in Monza.

the B&B Italia Research and Development Center, attended the same school, as did Paolo Nava, his colleague during his two years of teaching activity in 1971–72 and then his partner until the beginning of the eighties. In those years the art college in Cantù played a central role in the training of numerous designers who went on to work with manufacturers in Brianza.

Citterio's father was a small-scale craftsman-entrepreneur, and the majority of the people he knew and spent time with were connected in some way with the manufacturing of furniture. So his son found himself in the ideal environment to develop his aptitude for design in this sector.

The fact of his having grown up essentially "in the field" appears significant, because it has allowed him to develop, through concrete and firsthand experience, a keen understanding of some of the peculiarities at the base of the design and production of furniture.

An element that served to link individual situations and local entrepreneurial know-how was provided by the exhibitions that were staged in Brianza from the end of the fifties onward, such as the Mostre Selettive in Cantù (the first held in 1955), the Biennale dello Standard nell'Arredamento at Mariano Comense (which began in 1958), the Settimane Lissonesi and the Biennali in Carugo. For the young Citterio they represented an opportunity to keep abreast of new developments, as well as to put his own skills to the test, in particular through the design competitions associated with them, in which he participated toward the end of the sixties. In 1968 a piece of furniture with sheet-metal profiles, designed by Citterio with Vittorio Prato and Gianluigi Meroni, won a prize at the Carugo Biennale. In 1970 Citterio enrolled in the department of architecture at Milan Polytechnic, where he graduated in 1976 under Silvano Tintori with a thesis on the navigation of the Po River. He then continued along his own fairly personal course of training, little drawn to the climate of critical reflection on design and politico-cultural protest of the period and more interested in problems specific to the discipline of architecture. His years at university coincided with a phase of stylistic experimentation, conducted in part through his first

Renovation of the Piero
della Francesca room,
Pinacoteca di Brera,
Milan 1981, in collaboration
with Gregotti Associati.

Fausto Santini store, Florence,
1981.

collaborations with manufacturers in Brianza, and above all with a search for an approach to design that was essentially on the sidelines, and somewhat outside, the contemporary debate.

In his exploration of the masters of architecture (in addition to his study of rationalist works in Como and Milan, which he alternated with trips abroad to see buildings by Le Corbusier, Kahn and the Five Architects), the encounter with the work of Charles and Ray Eames remains fundamental. Among the attentive listeners at the public lectures that the ICF invited the two designers to give in Italy in 1968 was Citterio, who embarked on a thorough study of their furniture. This entailed making "life drawings" of the objects, focusing on their details as well as their structural solutions. A "journey of discovery" that reached its symbolic climax in 1984 when Citterio was taken by Rolf Fehlbaum of Vitra to meet Ray Eames (Charles had died some time earlier) at the designer's studio in California.

From 1972 to the early eighties he shared the studio in Monza with Paolo Nava, with whom he worked chiefly on design and exhibits. Citterio

was twenty when his first armchair, Poppy, designed for the 4P company and later sold at the La Rinascente department store as well, went into production in 1970. Poppy combined metal tubing and padding in a folding structure that fitted easily into the packaging made specially for it. In 1975 Citterio came up with an innovative design for a pen for Artvis. Although it never entered production, the pen had a soft central section that was easy to grip and anticipated a similar design that has been extremely successful in recent years.

During the seventies Citterio and Nava designed furniture for manufacturers in Brianza. With considerable determination, they sought collaborations with the larger manufacturers that would allow them to carry out interesting research into the product. In 1973 they started to work with B&B, passing from the Modulo 30 system (1973) to the Baia sofa (1975) and the Diesis (1979), the first complete example of an approach to design themes that were destined to become constants. In the meantime they developed other associations with companies like

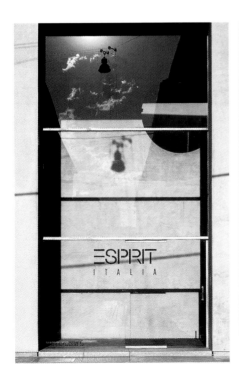

Esprit de Corp offices,
Via Forcella, Milan, 1985.

Max sofas, Flexform, 1983.

Flexform, Xilitalia, Boffi and Malobbia. Other products destined for success were Quadrante (1981) for Xilitalia and the Divani di Famiglia series (from 1980) for Flexform: the latter were influenced by the experience of an "educational" trip to the United States and an analysis of the furnishings of American lofts, characterized by understatement and informality.

At the beginning of the eighties the partnership with Nava came to an end. Citterio wanted to practice architecture too, and in the meantime carried on defining the characteristics of his personal understanding of design. The debate within the discipline, centering at the time chiefly on the activity of the Alchymia and Memphis groups and the emergence of a "new idea" of design, did not particularly interest the architect. "At the beginning of the eighties," he claims, "I had already found what I was looking for, my own road." While his studio was to remain in Monza until 1985, he moved his residence to Milan in those years, starting to spend more time with other designers and to experience the lively cultural climate of the Lombard capital. In 1981, as part of a general project of reorganization supervised by Vittorio Gregotti's studio, Citterio was asked by Pierluigi Cerri to collaborate on the renovation of the Piero della Francesca room at Brera, handled in a sober and rational style underlined by dry and incisive details and a specific attention to lighting.

The Fausto Santini fashion store in Florence dates from the same period, and would be followed over the years by the branches in Catania, Geneva, New York, Monaco, and Miami: a series of different sales outlets, but unified in the overall approach, where the products are made the most of by placing them in a clean spatial container. His first architectural project was Casa Busnelli, built between 1983 and 1986 for Piero Busnelli, the owner of B&B. This was a detached house that reinterpreted the rationalist style of the masters of Italian architecture in the years between the wars. Piero Busnelli was one of the first entrepreneurs to place his trust in the architect's talent, initiating an association that has lasted to the present day. Among the other industrialists Citterio has collaborated with are Pietro Galimberti of Flexform and Rolf Fehlbaum of Vitra, with whom he started to work in just those years. The architect has frequently pointed out the decisive role played by the client, by the continuity in time of professional and human relations, as well as by the need, in the creation of a global image for design companies, of a direct, unfiltered rapport.

In the mid-eighties, an important development was the beginning of his collaboration with Esprit de Corp—at the suggestion of Ettore Sottsass Jr., consultant to the chain of fashion stores at the time—that would culminate in the design of the Milan branch on Via Forcella, with offices, workshops and a showroom, and continue with other branches, like the one in Amsterdam. These interventions are characterized by a construction of essential and simple volumes/containers, in which the strong signals of the elements that articulate the work and service spaces are placed: from metal partitions to distinctive flights of stairs. Citterio recalls: "If I began to practice architecture, I owe it to Sottsass."

Ball point pens, Artvis, 1975.

Poppy armchair, 4P, 1970.

Diesis sofas, B&B Italia, 1979.

Divani di Famiglia sofas and armchairs, Flexform, 1980.

Antonio Citterio with the new generation of Italian designers, Milan, 1984.

1973

Modulo 30 seating system
B&B Italia
Antonio Citterio and Paolo Nava

Modulo 30 marked the beginning of Antonio Citterio and Paolo Nava's collaboration with B&B Italia. In 1966, assisted by its own research and development center, the company had started to experiment with the production of frames made out of polyester reinforced with glass fiber, a preimpregnate chosen from among the thermosetting substances available from the chemical industry because it possessed suitable properties of elasticity and resistance. Various designers—from Mario Bellini to Marco Zanuso and Joe Colombo—had tried their hands with this material in the past, studying the relationship between frame-container and padding in particular. The intention, utilizing the same hydraulic press as had been employed to make Mario Bellini's Amanta armchair, was to investigate the possibility of using this synthetic resin for the mass production of seating for public and communal spaces.

Taking their cue from this objective, the designers developed a system of seats based on the differentiated use of the same frame, and at the same time continued with the research into metal tubing already initiated by the R&D center. They eventually defined a simple U-shaped extruded structure (where great attention was paid to the point at which it bent, so as to prevent the seat from tipping over). Through die-cast joints, this supported the seat, made of plastic with a metal core and designed on a module of 30 centimeters.

Thus the theme of the project became the design of the junction between different materials. The various configurations of the system—from the single seat to the armchair and from seats set back-to-back to rows—are in fact possible using the same U-shape, the right way up or upside down, connected with two- or three-way right-angled joints. The upturned U forms the structure of the arm; a table of the same size as the base module can be set between two seats. Left more or less at the prototype stage, although the application of the same frame to revolving office chairs was studied, the system was limited to two substantial supply contracts: 1500 seats were produced for the basketball hall at Cantù, with a series of specially designed bars for fixing them to the tiers, while the possibility of a padding with "stockings" of polyurethane and Lycra was tried out for the renovation of the castle at Cozzo Lomellina.

1975

Baia sofa
B&B Italia
Antonio Citterio and Paolo Nava

The first of Antonio Citterio and Paolo Nava's designs for B&B Italia to go into mass production, Baia was also the first piece of padded furniture with a removable cover to be made by the company. Given that the object was intended from the outset for sale at a moderate price, and thus for wide-scale distribution, the rationalization of the constituent elements was the main problem faced in its design. Fully exploiting the technological resources available, and in particular the production line with a "Mammut-card" quilting machine, the designers conceived a system composed of just two basic seats and a simple and soft quilt.

They devised a covering in one piece, closed with a zip, starting out from the cut of the fabric, since the quilting, worked while flat, had to be designed in such a way that it assumed a three-dimensional form on the structure. This covering, made of fabric or leather and easy to remove, sheathed a cold-foamed padding supported by a framework, initially made out of vacuum-molded ABS and then metal, as this proved cheaper.

The process of reduction in the number of pieces related above all to the design of the parts of the sofa, which in fact consists of two modular portions with identical pieces forming the back and the arm, which folds to become a cushion.

Diesis sofas and armchairs
B&B Italia
Antonio Citterio and Paolo Nava

"Citterio was the youngest," recalls Piero Busnelli. "At the time we began to collaborate, important and established designers like Afra and
Tobia Scarpa, Mario Bellini, Vico Magistretti,
Gaetano Pesce and Marco Zanuso were working
for us. He turned up with a model of his first sofa
and it has all been fairly easy since. And then we
were from the same town…" He continues: "The
Diesis, for example, was created very quickly.
We moved rapidly from a first drawing to the
complete development of the product, as everything had been designed down to the tiniest details, allowing us to go straight into production."
Antonio Citterio and Paolo Nava devised a seating system based on the structural principle of
separation between the supporting and supported parts, in which each element clearly declares its function.

Diesis is characterized visually by the contrast
between the slenderness of the metal supporting structure, extremely controlled in its design
like the whole of the structural part, and what it
lifts above the ground: seat, back and arms
formed of stuffed cushions of traditional appearance, so neutral that they hardly look as if
they have been designed.

All of the structure's loads are supported by two
elements made of die-cast aluminum with a lentic-
ular section, whose reduced size is partly due to
the insertion of a bar of perforated steel during
the manufacturing process, with the aim of increasing the elastic strength of the leg. This work
of product engineering, initiated in 1973 for designs by Afra and Tobia Scarpa, continued the
studies carried out by the B&B Italia Research
and Development Center into die-cast pieces.

These elements ensure the stability of the entire
system, supporting the surfaces on which the
seat and arm are set and linking together the
structure of the back. The underseat is formed
of a blade with a triangular profile, obtained by
the coupling of two steel plates, fixed to two
crosspieces and set back from the front line of
the seat to reduce its visual impact.

The back, like the cantilevered shelf of the cush-
ion-arm, is a panel made of two die-formed layers
of hide stiffened and rendered elastic by a comb
of bundles of steel wire, which act as springs.

The same care over ensuring that the choice of
technological solutions and the handling of details respond to the requirements of functionality, durability and the capacity to make the whole

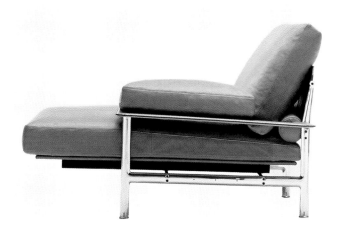

thing both light and sturdy is reserved for the cushions, "deliberately little designed with respect to the structure." Padded with polyurethane and sterilized goose feathers, they have removable covers of fabric or leather. In the latter case the leather on the back has micropores to make the most of the feather stuffing: when a weight is placed on them, air is expelled from the cushions and they deflate; when the weight is removed they do not remain squashed but return easily to their original shape. While this treatment of the material is intended to increase the comfort of the user, it also takes on a decorative role. Subsequently several modifications were made to the dimensions, structure and materials of the first model. The parts cast from brass, like the feet, were replaced with aluminum and hide agglomerate was associated with the leather, with the aim of eliminating any difference between the coverings of the structure and the padded part.

The range consists of a two- or three-seat sofa, with or without arms, an armchair and a chaise-longue with an arm on the right or left, and is completed by a corner table, a service shelf covered with leather and a single table.

The final form of the Ialea chair, designed by Citterio and Nava in 1980 as a natural complement to Diesis, derived from a reflection on the design of the details used to integrate different materials.

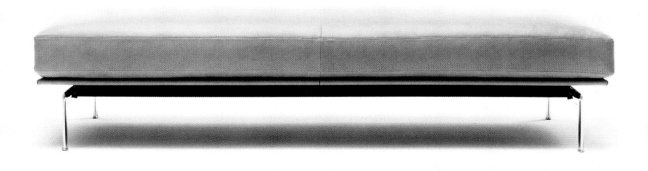

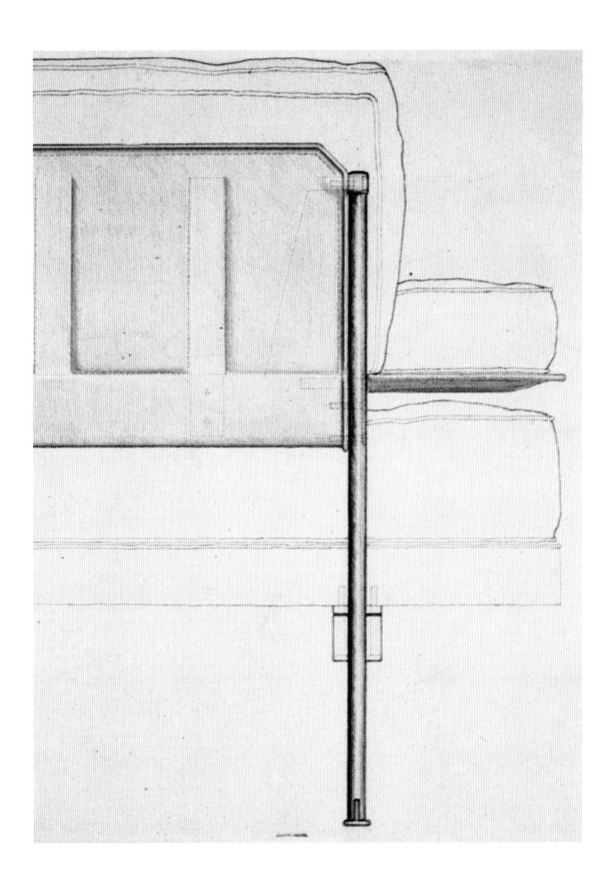

Divani di Famiglia sofas and armchairs, Flexform

1980, Doralice, Filiberto, Antonio Citterio
and Paolo Nava; 1985, Nonnamaria

"It is a question of not just physical but also emotional comfort, like a hug." This is what Citterio and Nava declared in 1980, when presenting this series of sofas and armchairs with names clearly alluding to a family context: Doralice, Filiberto, Ugomaria and Gino. The evident and somewhat ironic citation of models drawn from memory—such as a chair designed by his father and later covered, which he had always seen at home—is the cue for designing objects that seem timeless, as if they had been present forever. This aspect of duration, in addition to the discreet and balanced proportion of the forms, hinges on the total removability of the covering that enfolds them, and is reminiscent of those family "heirlooms" that have been covered to make them last longer and that are renovated every now and then by replacing the covers. Their practicality, comfort and sturdiness derive from the structural solutions and the materials utilized. Another important influence on this project came from the lofts Citterio visited in the United States, mostly created inside former industrial buildings and furnished with understated and informal armchairs and sofas, frequently covered with cloth to give them new life. In all the models the wooden structure is hidden under the padding of polyurethane wrapped in protective fabric and then by a cloth cover, easily replaceable as it is fixed with Velcro. Ugomaria is the redesign of a classic upholstered sofa, with cozy forms and a roundish arm and a back and seat formed of comfortable feather cushions with a crush-proof internal support. The last piece, designed by Citterio alone and produced by Flexform since 1985, is Nonnamaria, where the profiles are slimmed down by eliminating the cushions from the back; the chaise-longue was added to the range later.

It was with the Aria and Pasodoble sofas (both designed with Nava) in 1979 that Citterio had commenced his collaboration with Flexform, a company which had already worked with designers like Joe Colombo and Cini Boeri. The association with Citterio was destined to last, involving the design of furniture and the determination of overall strategies, such as the decision to bring back into production objects by rationalist architects like Mario Asnago, Claudio Vender and Gabriele Mucchi, in what can be considered a homage to the masters of the architect from Brianza.

DORALICE

NONNAMARIA

DORALICE

Factory kitchens
Boffi
Antonio Citterio and Paolo Nava

With Factory, Citterio and Nava proposed a model of kitchen that was new in its conception of the use and organization of space inside and outside the unit, adapting for the home (partly with a view to keeping prices low) industrially produced equipment and accessories hitherto neglected in this area and used for other purposes. They associated these elements with familiar materials like wood, copper, steel and fabric, proposing spatial, material and ergonomic solutions capable of making the kitchen a discreet, rigorous but pleasant presence in the house.

It is not the individual containers of the system that are fixed to the wall, but their backs. Onto these are anchored the shelves, not just making mounting rapid and easy but allowing the storage units to take up very little space. In addition, since only the backs rest on the floor, the units are raised completely above the ground, facilitating cleaning. A wide range of solutions are available to close the containers, including laminate doors, plastic-coated rolling shutters and panels of fabric (in bright colors, removable and washable) on metal frames, all designed to make work in the kitchen easier. For the hatch doors, for example, a friction hinge, patented by Boffi, is used to block the door at the desired height. This allows whoever is preparing the food not only to see what is in the containers, but also to move around rapidly without open doors getting in the way. Sliding doors of wired glass define the area of the larder, which has pull-out drawers on wheels in the lower part, and at the same time provide access to the space in the corners, usually out of reach or hard to use. Grilles of chrome-plated steel wire, of industrial origin, constitute the shelves and internal partitions of the units. "Decorated" steel unifies work surfaces, cooking range and sink, as well as climbing up the wall to form the front panel. The Factory collection is completed by the Toscano table and Le Rosette chairs, which have the same characteristics of essentiality and rigor.

Inspired by the informal atmosphere and furnishings of the lofts seen by Citterio on his trips to the United States at the end of the seventies, Factory has undergone various modernizations and remains in production today.

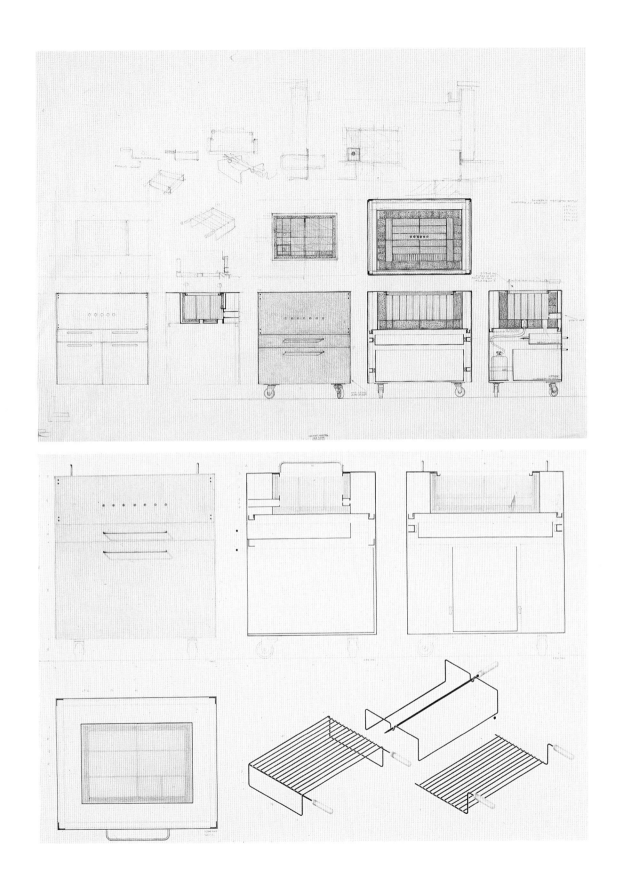

Quadrante range of furniture
Xilitalia-B&B Italia
Antonio Citterio and Paolo Nava

One of the strongest influences on Citterio's professional formation came from the Italian school of rationalism. The Quadrante series (named after the architectural magazine of the same name founded by Pier Maria Bardi and Massimo Bontempelli in 1933), designed by Citterio and Nava, took its inspiration in particular from the furniture of Mario Asnago and Claudio Vender exhibited at the 6th Milan Triennale in 1936.

Made by Xilitalia, the division of B&B Italia devoted to the production of lacquered furniture, Quadrante constitutes a true program of furnishing, comprising containers with sliding doors of various sizes and a table, designed to function both as individual objects and in coordination with a system of fitted walls that defines the limits of the room, serving as a backdrop for the pieces of furniture.

In the storage units, characterized by a horizontal subdivision, the expressive and chromatic values of the lacquer and glass are heightened by the radical simplification of the forms and the strict control over execution. In particular, the cabinet framed by a slender border of wood lacquered with shiny waterproof polyester has transparent panes of glass at the front and back as well as shelves of the same material. This visual permeability, which generates a continuous dialogue between the contents and the surrounding space, is

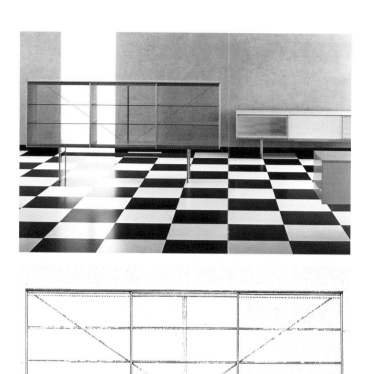

accentuated by the supporting structure of almost invisible track-beams, on which slide the large doors at the front, bordered with profiles of pale and shiny anodized aluminum. The same metal is used for the backs and the pair of legs, with adjustable feet. Given stability by slender steel tie rods at the back, the cabinet uses a sophisticated structural system that allows volumes and thicknesses to be reduced to a minimum and the use of large expanses of glass and unobtrusive metal components. "The architectural approach in this project lies in the work on the structures," Citterio has declared, "in tackling the concept of the supporting and supported parts, and in emphasizing the horizontal elements, the 'beams,' the joints, in which each piece possesses a functional definition of its own."

The low unit and bookcase are closed by drawers and retractable and sliding doors of lacquered wood and transparent, frosted or cobalt blue glass, while the fitted walls, also made of lacquered plywood, permit great flexibility of use since they are made to measure. Advanced technological and manufacturing solutions have been developed for the supporting structure that, among other things, make it easy to assemble and fix the parts. The design is couched in an uncompromising and extremely refined language, which succeeds in giving concrete expression to the distinctive aesthetics of rationalism, aimed at giving structure to the objects while taking away their substance and physicality.

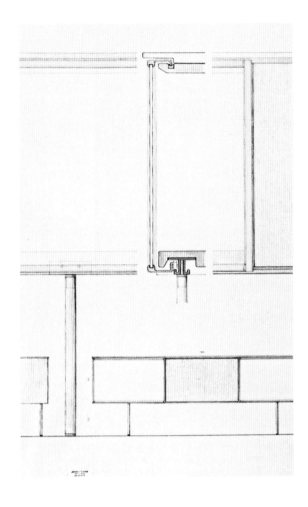

Sofas and chaise-longue, Flexform

1982, Magister sofa, Antonio Citterio
and Paolo Nava;
1983, Max and Phil sofas with Myriam Veronesi;
1985, Ginger sofa and chaise-longue

In the padded furniture he designed for Flexform
in the first half of the eighties, Citterio took his cue
from structural and formal typologies and solutions dating from the early decades of the twenti-
eth century, and from objects made of metal tubing in particular, and tried to incorporate contemporary uses and values into them.

Magister, a sofa designed in 1982, belongs to the
rationalist line inaugurated with the Quadrante system. Standing on slender cylindrical metal legs, it
contains, within a covered U-shaped structure of
the same thickness, seat and back padded in
polyurethane and Dacron with a quilted fabric or
leather covering and cylindrical arms stuffed with
feathers. Its distinctive feature is the retractable
shelf at the back: made of perforated sheet metal
and used to hold glasses, books and the like during conversation, it can be raised to give the seat
greater depth and allow the sofa to be converted
into a bed. It is a functional mechanism of refined
design that is invisible when viewed from the front.

In 1983 Citterio designed Max and Phil, matching
sofas that set out to re-create the atmosphere
of the private clubs of some European cities, ob-
served in pictures of interiors from the thirties. Intended to provide "places" for comfortable conversation, they stand in space as individual objects,

MAGISTER

breaking free from the customary position against the wall. Structurally they continue the reflection initiated with Diesis on the relationship between supporting and supported elements, associating it here with a curved and precisely designed form, that extends to seat and back. In Max the frame of chromed or satin metal is exposed to view, rising at three points to hold a dynamic cylindrical back padded with polyurethane and covered in a fabric with a stripe that forms a spiral pattern. This "winding" of the fabric not only makes it possible to cover the back without revealing the stitching, but also to distance the object from its historical reference, not without a touch of irony. Thus the stripes and the rounded form create a deliberate contrast with the style of reference. The seat of the Phil sofa, on the other hand, is contained within a high, solid border, padded and upholstered, that embraces it and descends slightly below the lower edge. Specific and substantial feather cushions increase the level of comfort.

Two years later Citterio came up with Ginger, a sofa and chaise-longue alluding to the models of the Bauhaus but designed to suit more up-to-date patterns of behavior, such as relaxing, eating and watching television. A seat in polyurethane foam and a back stuffed with feathers are supported by a linear framework of chrome-plated steel tubing which, in the position of the arm, at the end of the segment that bends to form the front legs, holds a revolving chrome-plated or leather-covered oval table.

MAGISTER

MAGISTER

MAX

GINGER

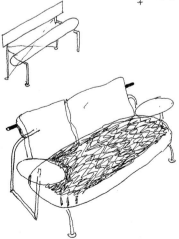

Milano coffee and tea service
Anthologie Quartett

From the outset the hallmark of the German
company Anthologie Quartett, founded by Rainer
Krause in 1983, has been its collaboration with
designers, especially the Memphis group head-
ed by Ettore Sottsass Jr. Citterio designed a
coffee and tea service in which all the pieces
are based on the form of the sphere and hemi-
sphere, playing with the combination of pure
volumes. The strictly white color of the hand-
crafted porcelain underlines the purity of the
geometry, which extends to the design of the details, from the handles to the spouts, giving the
objects a pleasingly familiar appearance.
Made up of several pieces (coffee-teapot, cups
and saucers, milk jug, sugar bowl and dishes for
cakes), it is one of the designer's rare ventures
into the sector of household articles.

Metropolis wall container
Tisettanta

Like the almost contemporary Sity range of padded furniture and the earlier Factory kitchen designed for Boffi at the end of the seventies, Metropolis is the fruit of a reflection carried out by the designer on the new functions demanded from furnishings as a consequence of changes in lifestyle. In the Metropolis system Citterio inserted a television set and hi-fi into the container: a recognition that electronic devices had become new cult objects and that the home and domestic life were increasingly centered on them. This was combined with the awareness of a transformation underway in the modes and organization of the manufacturing process at Tisettanta (a company set up in 1970 and interested in further developments in the field of industrial design after the experiments it had conducted with other designers) that were having an effect on aspects of design: the shift, that is, from the construction of a completely finished, even if modular, piece of furniture in the factory to the assembly of its parts. Given the company's considerable capacities in the area of industrial engineering, the architect focused his research on innovative technological solutions for a piece of furniture conceived as an integrated system of panels and mechanisms.

Definable as a wall system supported from the back, Metropolis is essentially characterized by a rigorous modular structure of uprights and crosspieces that form open or closed containers, adaptable to fit different lengths and heights of wall. In it is set a sort of gateway designed to hold the television and hi-fi systems and fitted with electricity outlets. A number of unprecedented functional and aesthetic elements have been introduced, such as the metal bar fixed on the front that serves as a support for the sliding doors and for the ladder. Its careful design is inspired by the ones used in libraries, allowing it to slide along the entire surface.

The highly flexible system, in production since 1984, has seen additions and variations over the course of time to adapt it to the public's changing needs and tastes. These include glass doors and containers of different depths fitted with drawers and various types of shutters or paneling used to form spacious open niches, in numerous color schemes.

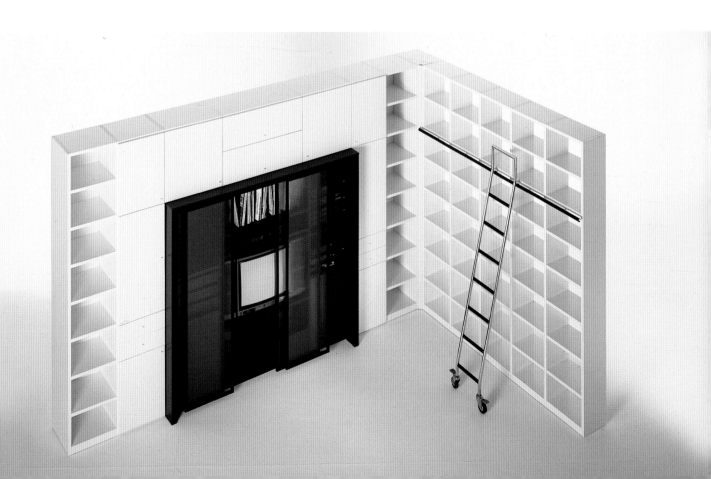

03

1986–99. product, system and "global" design

The mid–eighties was an important time of transition for Citterio, from the viewpoint of both quality and quantity: on the one hand it brought an increase in the number of architectural commissions and, on the other, the conquest of a precise identity and force—in the broad sense a "bargaining power"—in his design work with companies. Nor should we forget a number of physical, organizational and in a sense "cultural" changes linked to the opening of his studio on Via Maroncelli in Milan in 1986 and to his collaboration with the American architect Terry Dwan, who was to become his partner in life and work and whose presence, among other things, has helped to widen his international contacts and professional opportunities.

Over the fifteen years up to 2000 Citterio carried out several architectural projects, such as the renovation of the Esprit Benelux offices in Antwerp (1988), the Vitra manufacturing plant at Neuenburg (1992) and at Weil am Rhein (1992 and 1994), the Antonio Fusco factory at Corsico (1993) and a number of projects in Japan, including the experimental residential building at Kumamoto (1989) and the Ohbayashi offices and showroom (1991) and the head office of the Daigo Company (1992), both in Tokyo.

Citterio also designed showrooms for brands in the clothing industry, like Esprit and Fausto Santini. Toward the end of the nineties these were followed by showrooms for Cerruti (Milan, 1996; Moscow, 1998; New York, 1999), Alberto Aspesi (Milan, 1998) and Emmanuel Ungaro (Paris, 1999). In this period the architect also devoted himself to the creation of sales outlets for furniture manufacturers, including Vitra, B&B Italia, Ansorg, Arclinea and Habitat. Finally, he was responsible for the concept and image of the Smart Car showrooms (1998).

In particular, the designs of commercial premises developed his aptitude for the problems of the relationship between product and consumer, investigating the significance and the modes of use and perception of contemporary merchandise. These skills led him to reflect on the changes that had taken place in the market, moving him implicitly in the direction of a progressive expansion of the designer's modes

Stand for B&B Italia, Salone del Mobile, Milan, 1986.

of intervention. In essence, Citterio developed a flexible approach to the design of the industrial product, inserting it increasingly into the context of the company's overall strategy and thus looking not just at questions of design, technology and production, but also at those of communication, marketing and distribution. Thus he focused his attention on the whole gamut, from the individual object to systems, and from the product in its entirety to the integral and integrated design of spaces.

The product that symbolizes the change of tack in the mid-eighties is the Sity sofa for B&B: a system of furnishing for the living area that has not found easy acceptance, but that introduced the innovative typological variant of the "island" structure, destined to prove popular. This proposal was the result of his observation of changes in ways of life and living which were making the sofa a crucial piece of furniture, undergoing continual transformations in its use: no longer a static element of the bourgeois drawing room, it had become an object with many possible functions, the physical and visual center of the space. Its commercial and critical success (Sity was awarded the Compasso d'Oro in 1987) undoubtedly made a significant contribution to the growth of his prestige among manufacturers. The architect has worked for a long time on the idea of the sofa-island, in a personal process of refinement that, despite the variations in the language adopted, has continued in essence right up to his most recent products, such as Harry, Charles and Marcel.

Over the course of thirty years Citterio has worked with two generations of Busnelli entrepreneurs: Piero (founder of C&B, later B&B) and then his son Giorgio, whom he had known personally since his youth. Citterio's collaboration with B&B can be divided into two distinct periods of time and levels of involvement: up until the mid-nineties, when he was certainly one of its most important designers with successful products like Diesis and Sity to his credit; and subsequently, when he assumed a wider role, at once that of inspirer and interpreter of a global idea of the company. "Since 1994 he has been our architect of reference," confirms Giorgio Busnelli.

Advertisement for Sity, B&B Italia, 1986.

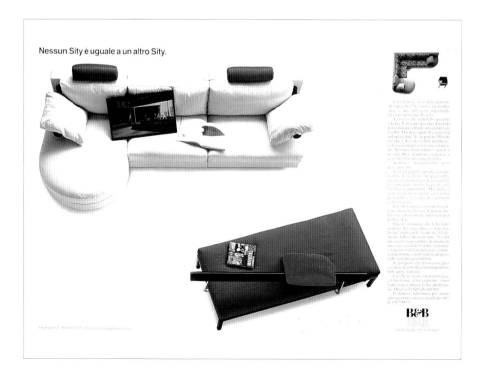

"Before, we had a catalogue made up of products with many different spirits, but with Citterio we have arrived at a uniform and consistent line, into which the products of other designers are able to fit harmoniously too. We have changed from being a company of soloists into one with a conductor." He now plays a part in many areas of the company's activity, devoting himself to product, exhibit and retail design. This all-round involvement is bolstered by a constant dialogue with the management and with the company's research and development center (whose premises have recently been renovated to Citterio's design), fundamental to B&B's method of working since it allows B&B to carry out careful studies, develop concepts and try out structural solutions and details. In addition, Citterio has made a precise contribution to opening up the manufacturer to the possibilities of international projects, with the aim of getting in tune with what is going on in the world of contemporary design.

Alongside the partnership with B&B, he established links with many other Italian and foreign manufacturers, some of them destined to last.

Since the mid-eighties Citterio has worked with Vitra on several architectural projects and on the Vitrashop-Visplay display systems for shops, sales points and department stores: an intervention couched in terms of an industrial methodology and a basic language, capable of responding in full to technical and functional requirements, as well as that of economies of production. At the same time Citterio has continued to produce designs for the office, from chairs to furnishing systems. He first turned his attention to lighting with technical equipment for Ansorg, a company belonging to the Vitra group. These objects were characterized by a marked interest in problems of lighting technique, combined with an approach to their design that brought them closer to models for the home. He took the same approach to the technical products for Flos, with which he started to collaborate at the end of the nineties: the objects he designed for the company covered a broad spectrum of research, with results that differed widely, as in the case of the innovative hanging lamp Lastra (1998) or the Kelvin table model (2003).

Advertisement for Charles, B&B Italia, 1998.

B&B Italia. La scelta della qualità, dell'armonia e del vivere contemporaneo.

Charles, divano di sedute e. Antonio Citterio.
Per conoscere il Rivenditore più vicino, componete il numero verde 167-018370. Internet: http://bebitalia.it

B&B ITALIA
Qualcosa che vale nel tempo

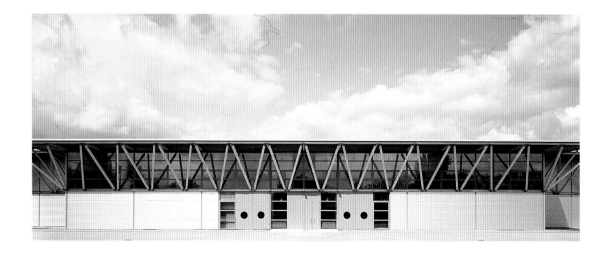

In the field of furniture, while continuing his collaboration with manufacturers like Flexform in a process of ever closer identification, the architect was engaged on other fronts. He reexamined the concept of bookcases, storage units and fitted walls with Domus (1989) for B&B. With Kartell he explored the use of synthetic materials, proposing traditional typologies, like those of the small table or trolley, in a contemporary key, but without losing their character as familiar and reassuring products.

In the second half of the nineties he tackled the area of bathroom design, first for Inda and then for Pozzi Ginori and Axor, taking an essentially systemic approach, just as he had already done with the Arclinea kitchens at the end of the eighties. The aim was to configure the whole space in an all-inclusive and coordinated way, passing from a logic based on individual elements to a comprehensive line of attack intended to give the maximum dignity to the use of materials, technologies and formal solutions.

Citterio also ventured into spheres of design different from furnishing, commencing with his work for companies applying advanced technology, such as the computer for Max Data (1997), the studies for Brionvega television sets (1999) or the research into the interiors of Alfa Romeo automobiles (2000).

The architect explored yet another field in his successful design of hospital structures for Malvestio (1992), which combined accuracy of technical and functional solutions and materials with an up-to-date language.

At the end of the nineties, the substantial increase in professional opportunities led to various changes in the organizational structure of his studio and its human resources. From the small number of assistants employed in Monza, Citterio's staff rose to around thirty people in these years, at the studio located on Via Maroncelli until 1991 and then on Via Lovanio, with a further increase in size in 2000 when it was moved to Via Cerva.

In 1984 Citterio also started to work with Patricia Viel, who became a partner in the architectural studio in 2000. In the field of industrial design, the German Glen Oliver Löw was an assiduous collaborator and coauthor of the majority of projects from 1985 to 2000. "His contribution has been very important to me," says Citterio. "In some ways we are complementary. He arrived when he was still a student at the Domus Academy. I needed someone whose mother tongue was German for my projects in Germany and Switzerland; he stayed in the studio for fifteen years. He has a very systematic and precise method of working, allowing him to concentrate on a project for a long time and examine every single aspect and detail in depth."

The broad typological and quantitative range of Citterio's interventions reflects a methodological versatility in the combination and exploitation of the productive, technological, commercial and distributive resources, as well as the human ones, present in the various companies he works with. A capacity for understanding of the context is placed at the service of a personal research that is ongoing and at the same time in tune with contemporary sensibility and with a new idea of product and consumption.

Citterio does not so much adopt a univocal language, the expression of a characteristic poetics that is displayed in a variety of ways, as a methodology that is recognizable and flexible at one and the same time.

AC 2 office chair, Vitra, 1990.

Ad Hoc office furniture system, Vitra, 1994.

Vitra furniture factory, Neuenburg, Germany, 1992.

Antonio Citterio and Terry Dwan's studio, Via Maroncelli, Milan, 1988.

Sity system of sofas
B&B Italia

The Sity system of sofas proposes a new type of seating, made up of disconnected and flexible parts, translating "the structure of comfort typical of the middle-class home," as Enrico Morteo points out, "into the modern language of its differentiated elements."

The design, which had been on the drawing board since the end of 1982 and had met some resistance in the commercial department of B&B Italia, not optimistic about the possibilities of its success, was presented at the 1986 Salone del Mobile of Milan in a setting devised by Antonio Citterio with Pierluigi Cerri.

Expanding on the research begun with Max and Phil in the same years and returning to an idea already put forward in Florence Knoll's sofas of the sixties, among others, Citterio introduced the principle of the "island" arrangement of seats into the living room, showing that it is possible to control the organization of space through the design of padded furniture. The system, totally disengaged from the walls and without any fixed location in the room, is based on the coordination of more than twenty formally and functionally independent pieces,

capable of furnishing rooms in a way that suits the needs of consumers always on the lookout for less restricted and more comfortable styles of living.

The availability of a wide range of solutions is associated with an alteration in the customary forms of the seats, which, like soft platforms, have curved surfaces reminiscent of Le Corbusier's designs and unusual depths and breadths, creating zones for conversation, nooks of solitary concentration and islands for relaxation.

"In Sity, the fact that the sofas were longer, wider or narrower," Citterio has commented, "was not just a formal or marketing choice, but an interpretation of daily life in the home. The sofa is no longer a piece of furniture on which people sit just to chat; in contemporary society you sit on the sofa and at the same time talk, eat, watch television, write."

Without abandoning the traditional pattern of the sofa seating two or three people and the single armchair, but integrating it with the concept of the chaise-longue, the system consists of a main nucleus of padded furniture for one or two people with a rectangular or rounded seat,

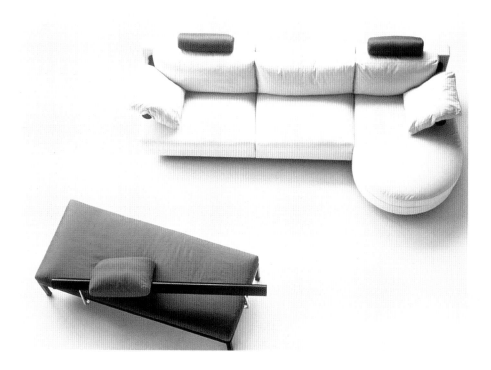

elongated or shaped with increasing depth, where the terminal elements are distinguished by a cantilevered tubular arm, covered in leather. On the arm is set a rectangular cushion that the designer conceives, returning to a reflection begun with Diesis, as a classic feather cushion on which to rest the head. All the elements have removable covers of fabric or leather, while the structure that supports them is made of steel section clad in cold-foamed polyurethane. The seat is padded with Dacron, while the cushions, backs and arms are stuffed with feathers.

Around this main nucleus are structured two other series of pieces, which use the same formal lexicon as the rest of the system: individual seats designed especially for rest that adopt the same circular arm but elongate it and even turn it into a revolving back, and a group of semirigid seats covered in leather without visible stitching, mounted on aluminum structures.

The Sity system, which won the Compasso d'Oro in 1987, has proved a great commercial success, and this is perhaps because, as Citterio says, "it is a 'different' but in the end 'normal' object, in the sense that it still resembles a sofa, and is comfortable; above all it interprets and satisfies the needs of a very broad section of the market."

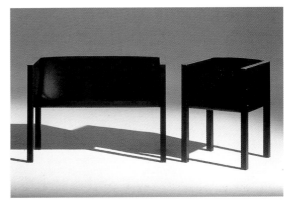

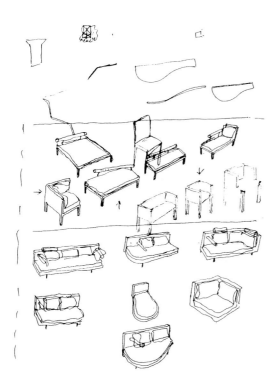

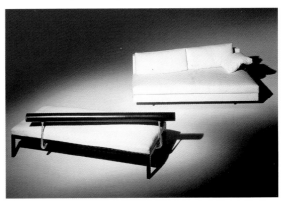

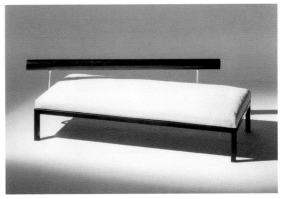

Kitchens, Arclinea

1988, Italia; 1992, Mediterranea; 1996, Artusi, Florida, Ginger; 2002, Convivium

In the middle of the eighties Citterio commenced several important collaborations that were destined to last in time, with manufacturers like Vitra, Kartell and Arclinea.

For the latter, a company based in Vicenza that had been producing modular kitchens since 1960, Citterio designed a series of models which had in common an attempt to resolve the general problems posed by the use of this area of the house. They did so by taking a unitary approach to working and living in the kitchen, developed through specific programs of research. One of the initial stimuli was an effort to understand how work is carried out in the kitchen, i.e. what are the necessary functions to which design needed to provide a response. The goal was a kitchen that would be at once "professional and domestic," where the work can easily be organized, everything is within reach and in view and the units are suited to containing, preparing and cooking food. Such a kitchen had to provide appropriate surfaces and a correct internal organization of movements and arrangement of the furniture, which is structured into individual and versatile blocks of steel, some of them free-standing.

The design of the appliances and their integration into the system as a whole have been other significant themes. "In those years," Citterio declares, "I worked continuously on several questions. In particular the relationship between household appliances and the kitchen: the choice of steel, which offers practical and functional advantages as well as an attractive appearance, essentially steered me toward the idea of a professional kitchen located in the home.

FLORIDA

ARTUSI

ARTUSI

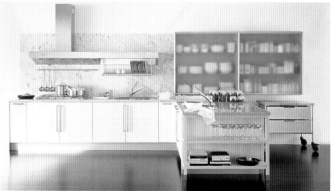

ARTUSI

CONVIVIUM

The kitchen is made up of surfaces and containers; the correct relationship between all these elements permits a rational utilization of the spaces. I came to design more than one model, one system, with individual elements that could be used separately and combined with each other, guided by the intention to create a setting increasingly integrated with the rest of the house."

As far as the appliances and their location in space are concerned, the Italia model already assigned them a functional and visual presence. Later they were proposed as an "island," serving as the physical center of the room. Finally, as in the Convivium series, they were placed in a more secluded and enclosed area, which was accompanied by an area for eating in order to generate an ever greater harmony with the other parts of the house.

Such developments in the logic of design are clearly related to changes in lifestyle, with the new central role of the kitchen, no longer a limited, specialized or technical area but an open place of interaction.

An approach that makes use of positive elements derived from an understanding of the kitchen interwoven with traditions, but totally reappraised from the viewpoint of the design of the individual elements of which it is made up, of their functionality and of the organization of the spaces.

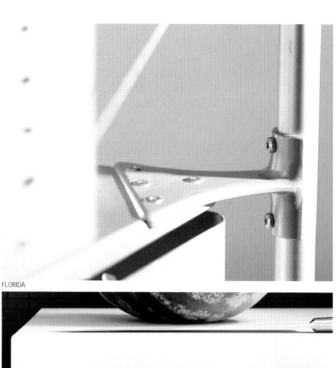

FLORIDA

FLORIDA

CONVIVIUM

CONVIVIUM

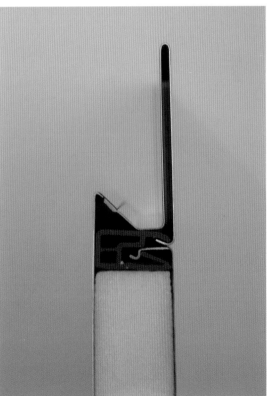

Domus system of fitted walls
B&B Italia

The idea of creating a structure of fitted walls
where horizontal modularity takes perceptual and
structural prevalence over the vertical one dates
back to 1987 and stemmed from the simple observation of a common system of rolling shutters
for stores. Combining this suggestion with the designer's "architectural" propensity to treat the various elements of the system as volumes in space,
the back, typical of the fitted wall, practically disappears from view and the appearance of the system changes, becoming glass cabinet, bookcase,
display stand… An emphasis that signals the shift
from the two dimensions of the wall to the three
dimensions of the piece of furniture, something
that is also well represented by the thickness giv-
en to the end pieces of the vertical containers.
Domus has been produced since 1989 by B&B
Italia, "the only company with which it was possible to make innovations in the typology of storage
units," explains Citterio, "precisely because it did
not come from that sector, 'suffering' at that time
from a considerable stagnation in production and
modes of distribution." Domus was designed to
offer a wide range of sizes and storage functions,
combinable with a number of base elements
whose measurements could be adapted to meet

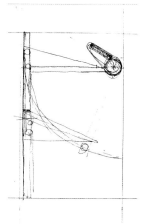
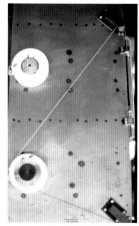

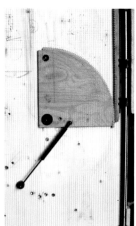

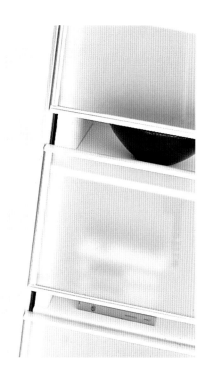

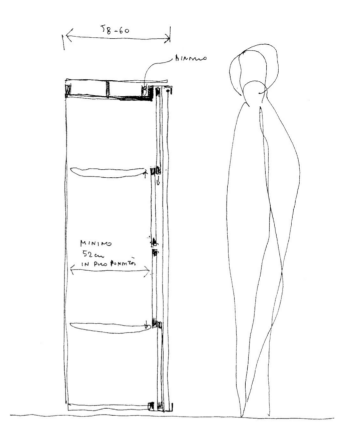

different individual requirements. The marked horizontality that focuses attention on the shutters, either panels or panes of glass, detaching it from the link with the walls, is permitted in part by the adoption of two significant technical and structural solutions developed by the B&B Italia Research and Development Center: the plastic tops, generally used for doors and windows or for outdoor furniture in imitation cane, and the rotation mechanism of the horizontal doors inserted in the backs. The choice, innovative in this sector, of rigid extruded and expanded PVC, an effective substitute for wood owing to its mechanical properties, resistance to atmospheric agents (water and dust), workability and cost, has made it possible to design painted tops with a winged section, visually unobtrusive but capable of reaching considerable lengths and supporting heavy weights without warping. Also, its hollow section means that it can be fitted with a metal core in the extrusion phase and house power cables and flush spotlights.

These shelves are supported by posts at the sides, onto which is fixed a special mechanism for the sliding doors patented by the company. Unlike other systems on the market, which are based on the use of counterweights and housed in the rear wall of the unit, reducing the space available, this mechanism is light and takes up little room. It is installed in the side wall and requires very little effort to operate, thanks to a sliding carriage connected to elastic elements capable of exerting a variable force of reaction that rebalances each position.

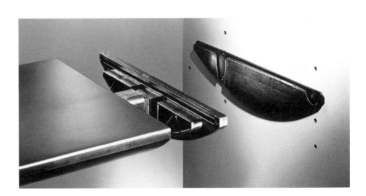

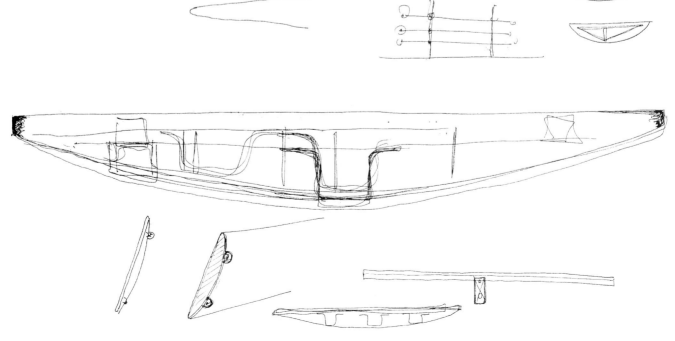

Draft Line drawing boards and work tables
Bieffe
with Sergio Brioschi and Glen Oliver Löw

Bieffe is a division of Bieffeplast specializing in the production of drawing boards. The company, founded in the early fifties, has worked with various designers over the course of time, commencing with Joe Colombo, whose classic Boby trolley (1971) it produced.

In 1989 Citterio, tackling the design of an instrument used in his own profession ("in practice an object designed for himself"), developed the Draft Line, made up of drawing boards and other items of furniture for design studios.

The series consists of a number of base elements, drawing boards and simple work surfaces that, combined with one another and with others, form groups of multifunctional work stations and are completed by containers and chests of drawers, some fitted with castors. In particular the tops, which can be fitted with tilting and raising devices or with light boxes, have characteristic arched legs at the back and can also be moved around on wheels.

A suitable response to the growing use of electronic devices is provided by special computer and printer stands with trays and tables for monitors. These are fitted with ducts that have a structure of metal tubing painted with epoxy powders in the colors black and aluminum gray, and with laminate or wooden tops with solid wood borders.

Draft Line marked the architect's first foray into the realm of furnishings for workspaces, a sector in which he was to work for a long time, commencing briefly with Olivetti and then, uninterruptedly, over a period of sixteen years with Vitra.

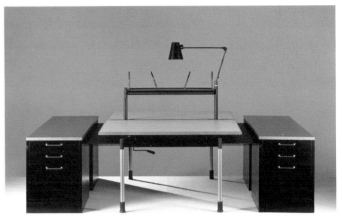

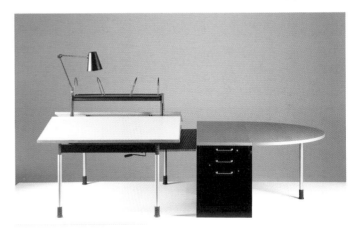

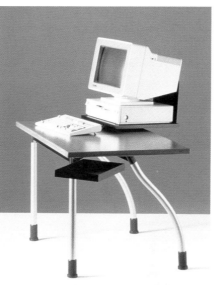

Ephesos office furniture
Olivetti Synthesis
with Sergio Brioschi

"When a leading company like Olivetti Synthesis proposes a new product, we expect to see something highly innovative and technologically astounding. One of the most surprising aspects of the new line of office furniture is the extraordinary ability with which the technological factor and the innovative element are expressed with the greatest morphological and structural simplicity." This is what Citterio had to say on the occasion of the presentation of the Ephesos office system, hinting at the key elements of his work. At the end of a long period of reflection on the organization of workspaces based on the open plan, Ephesos proposed the model of the Combi office, which integrated the individual workstation with common functions and space: small workspaces for one or two people, connected visually with an area used for activities that require larger numbers. A plan of operation made up of free-standing elements that can be freely combined in a variety of ways. The system turns on a small number of basic elements, the use of multifunctional panels, the structural solidity provided by sheet metal and a range of finishes in different colors that serve to distinguish the workstations. Among its interesting features are the decision to set the units on the worktop instead of on the ground, the attention paid to the passage of electric cables and the overall structure of square and geometric volumes that give the whole an essential and tidy air. The pieces of furniture are the result of a precise effort of design and production aimed at reducing costs, partly in relation to the specific nature of the Olivetti distribution network, which required objects that would be easy to arrange and install. The project took into consideration the characteristics of the organization of production, based on a relatively simple technology that could make use of techniques drawn from handicrafts, in particular the pressing of sheet metal. Olivetti Synthesis was set up in 1930 as a division of the Olivetti group specializing in the office furniture sector, and over the years had worked with important architects and designers, just as the mother company did with its typewriters and computers. It was also responsible for the visual design of the elements of the corporate identity. Olivetti has played a fundamental role in this country, partly thanks to the enlightened strategy pursued by Adriano Olivetti, who turned to the best architects of the time to design its production and service facilities and supported many scientific and cultural initiatives.

Fittings for department stores, Vitrashop-Visplay

1990, Cargo;
1999, Kado, Pick Up, with Glen Oliver Löw

The collaboration with Vitra embraced a wide range of areas of intervention, including display systems for sales points. This sector presents a number of specific features, such as the need to meet particular technical and functional requirements and exercise the maximum of control over manufacturing costs. It is a sphere in which it is important to keep the characterization of form to a minimum and focus instead on simplicity of construction and installation: an approach to design that has methodological parallels with the development of the anonymous object, not recognizable by any particular style but the outcome of a progressive refinement.

It is no accident that the development of the individual products has been conducted in an assiduous and continuous fashion over a long period of time. The same model has been perfected and updated in a process of continual fine-tuning.

Citterio's work, carried out in close collaboration with the company's technical department, is based on the concept of maximum flexibility of the individual constituent elements of the system to permit the creation of customized situations.

The first of these systems was Cargo, in which various functional accessories are mounted around a structure with a rack and two feet. The basis of the later Kado is a supporting structure in the form of a metal box, carefully defined and coupled with materials like satin glass and wood. Finally, Pick Up is characterized by an extreme visual lightness and the use of a simple metal structure.

In all the products great care has been taken over technical and structural details, whose design is essential, effective and clean. This is evident, for example, in the cross-shaped elements that contribute to the stability of the structure and in the systems for fixing and anchoring it to the ground or wall.

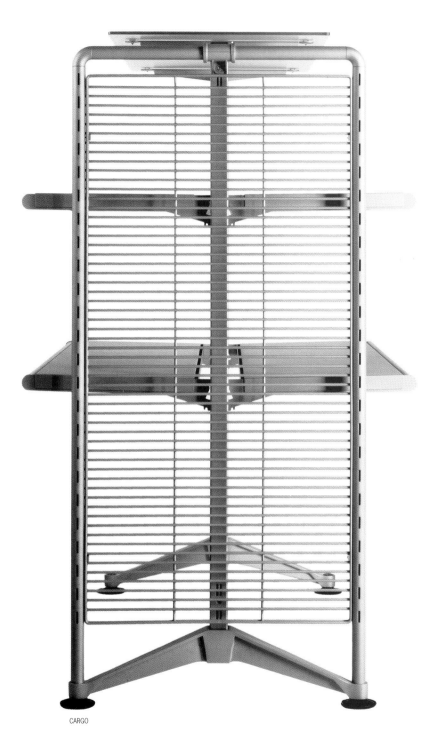

CARGO

 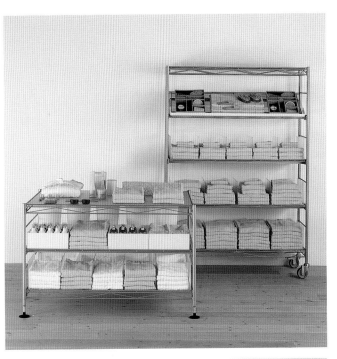

PICK UP

73

KADO

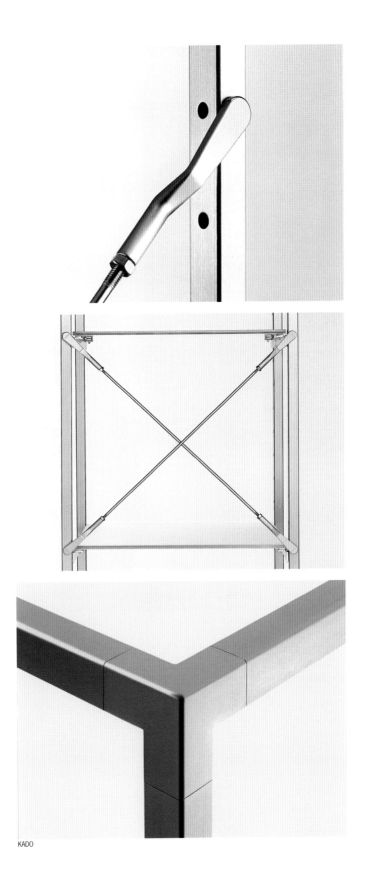

KADO

Adjustable chairs, Vitra

1990, AC 1, AC 2, Area;
1994, T-Chair, with Glen Oliver Löw;
1996, Axess, with Glen Oliver Löw;
2002, Oson C, Oson S

Citterio's collaboration with Vitra began in the mid-eighties and has continued to the present day with the development of seats and other furnishings for the office, as well as display and lighting systems and sales outlets. These are sectors characterized by a specialized approach, where considerable importance is attached to technical and production factors and the design process needs to address the requirements of standardized construction, in order to come up with products that are efficient and yet couched in a contemporary language.

Vitra is a fairly anomalous enterprise, which has expanded its range of interests over the course of time, eventually developing an overall strategy that embraces cultural aspects as well, and that has found concrete expression in the elaboration of instruments operating on different scales. For the architectural design of its own production and commercial facilities, the company has turned to some of the greatest contemporary architects (such as Frank O. Gehry, Zaha Hadid, Tadao Ando, Alvaro Siza and Citterio himself). It has also set up the Vitra Design Museum, which houses a collection of furniture and stages important exhibitions: a farsighted vision in which the institution is regarded both as a place for the protection, conservation and enhancement of the historical legacy and as a framework for reflection and debate on the culture of design.

Vitra has been producing the furniture of Ray and Charles Eames, George Nelson and Verner Panton under license since the seventies. It has always been the company's intention to have different forms of expressions hold a dialogue in its catalogue rather than to adopt a homogeneous language, a uniform style. Where the office is concerned, Vitra has sought an approach to design that would be able to break away from a predominantly technical and functionalistic tradition, drawing on the services of Italian designers as well, from Mario Bellini to Alberto Meda.

With Citterio the company has moved in the direction of the design of products, at first for retail and then for the office, that are simplified in their structure and manufacture and yet distinguished by innovative features. "We started to work with Antonio Citterio," recalls the firm's owner Rolf Fehlbaum, "because we were looking for a simpler language, an essential and

AC 1

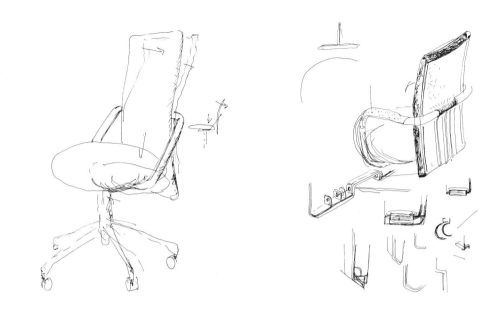

AC 1

effective mode of design. With AC 1, for example, we came up with a really new product, the result of a radical simplification of the chair as object that introduced, among other things, an unprecedented separation of seat and back." Since then the architect has been constantly involved in the development of the company's projects. "Citterio is someone capable of helping you produce large numbers. He has a very rare ability to grasp the needs of a manufacturer as well as to guarantee a constant quality of work, oriented not so much to a single product, but to a global design." And Fehlbaum continues: "With him we have progressively adopted a logic of product design, based on work on technologies, on new functional and typological solutions. He is extremely balanced in his design, so that he never comes up with a purely formal result. In his case it is interesting to look at the process that lies behind his projects, the result of a methodology rooted in both problem solving and commercial thinking, because he is thoroughly familiar with the whole procedure of industrial design."

The first office chair, produced in 1990, was AC 1, based on a geometric structure, especially that of the back, physically detached from the seat even in terms of functionality. The objective was to create a more slender rear support of square shape, contrasting with the soft and rounded seat. The back and arms are integral with one another and allow the sitter to move, adapting to his or her posture. In AC 2 the system of adjustment has been concealed inside

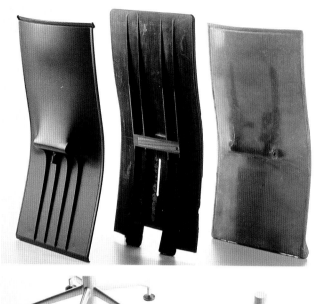

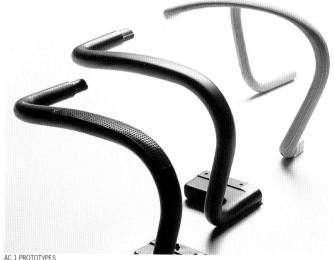

AC 1 PROTOTYPES

AC 1

the seat, giving the chair an extremely clean
and elegant appearance. An elegant and carefully designed structure of five inclined spokes
was adopted for the foot. "In the office chair,"
Citterio explains, "the technical component is
fundamental; in this case there is a great deal
of inventiveness linked with the mechanical aspect. Those were the years in which I was also
working on the mechanisms of the Domus storage unit for B&B and developing a more thorough understanding of the processes of industrial production. And they were also the years in
which the use of plastic components was becoming established, and computer programs
were beginning to be applied in design." In this
connection, Vitra collaborated with Du Pont on
evaluating the thickness and ribbing of the plastic (Derlin thermoplastic resin) used for the
back, going on to integrate this with research
carried out through models and prototypes.
Enrico Morteo wrote about the AC 1 chair in
Domus: "Citterio has chosen to go down the
road of refined technological research, with a
view to obtaining a radical simplification of the
object. Starting out from the idea of making the
back itself the spring that elastically controls
the movements of the structure, he has worked
on two points in particular. On the one hand the
search for a material suited to the purpose and
the development of an adequate structural design. On the other the study of a geometry as
simple as it is efficient." This research was also
related to a sustainable approach to the product, attentive to the question of dismantling its
parts for recycling and reuse. In fact looking at
the whole life cycle of the object constituted a
stimulus and a challenge for designer and industry, and was a sensibility that Citterio developed
in his collaboration with the Swiss manufacturer.
The work on office seating has continued over
the years with other models that, always derived from complex and wide-ranging studies,
respond to precise needs. A successful example of this appears to be the T-Chair model, with
its use of a new technology for the production
of an unstitched but three-dimensional fabric, allowing the object to be characterized by a novel
covering of the back with horizontal stripes.

AC 2

AC 2

AREA

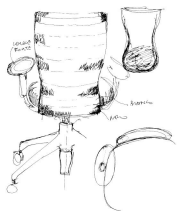

T-CHAIR

T-CHAIR

OSON C

OSON S

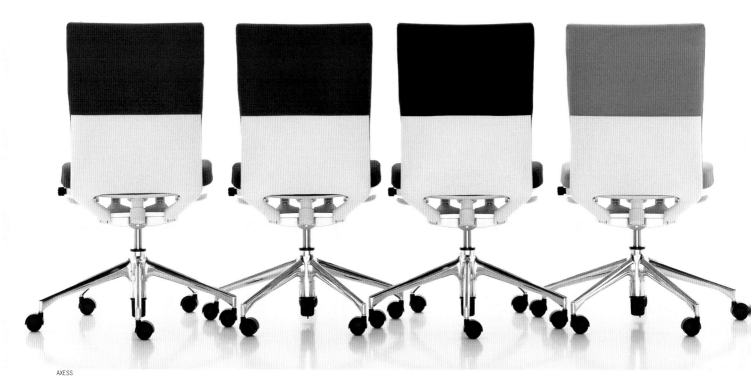

AXESS

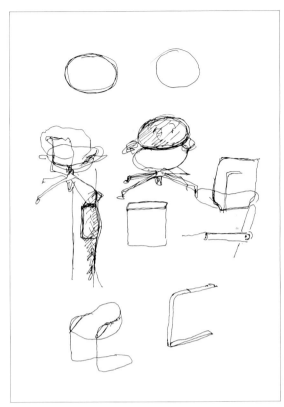

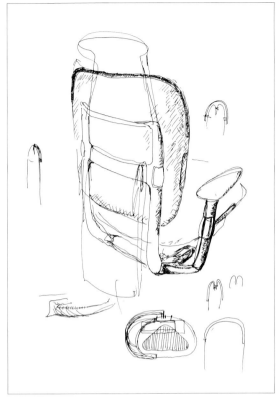

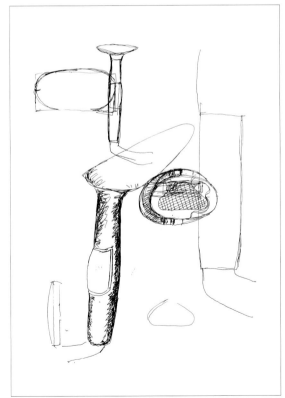

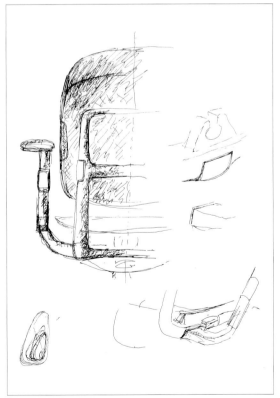

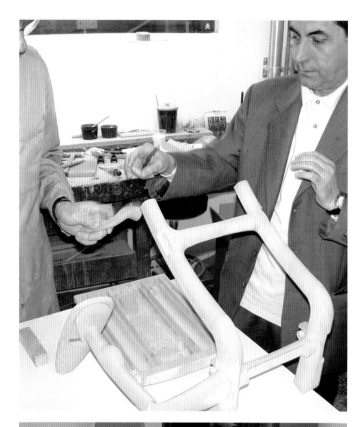

RESEARCH FOR BACKS OF OSON CHAIRS

Office chairs, Vitra

1992, Visaroll;
1992, Visavis, with Glen Oliver Löw;
2002, ToniX, with Toan Nguyen

Developed in the 1930s, the cantilevered tubular steel chair is a type of seating able to make
the technical and structural potentialities of the
material visible and tangible: a stable and elastic result hard to obtain with other materials.
In comparison with traditional cantilever designs (which Citterio himself has reinterpreted
with the AC 3 model for Vitra), Visavis intro-
duces several innovations: in the first place the
back is independent of the seat, whose suspen-
sion is made stable by the adoption of a special type of welding derived from other areas of
technology and use; in addition it utilizes a mix-
ture of materials, uniting the steel tubing with
the polypropylene of the back. This is a choice
aimed at attaining a high degree of elasticity

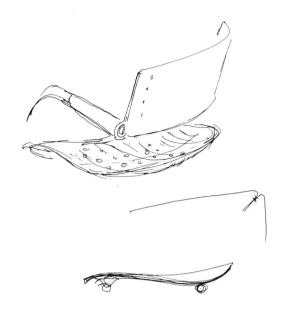

VISAVIS

and ergonomic response to the stresses to which those who sit and rest their back on it are subjected. At the same time, the use of single-component materials allows the chair to be dismantled for recycling and reuse.

The Visaroll version with casters adopts the same solution for the plastic back. In this model the back legs, again made of slender steel tubing, bend to become arms on which the back is inserted. The back is characterized by a pattern of square holes that makes it look lighter despite its structural solidity.

This last prototype can be linked with the recent ToniX, characterized by a single plastic piece that, inserted onto the rear supports, connects the comfortable flat arm and the elastic back.

Visavis is an object emblematic of the course followed by Citterio, and one rewarded by considerable commercial success: over a million of them have been produced.

VISAVIS

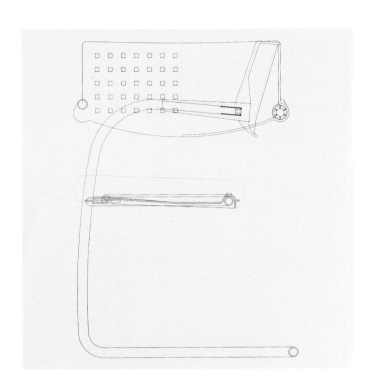

VISAROLL

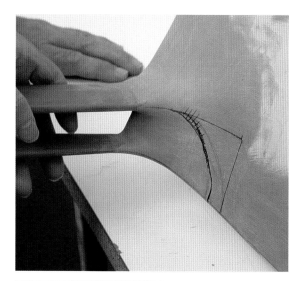

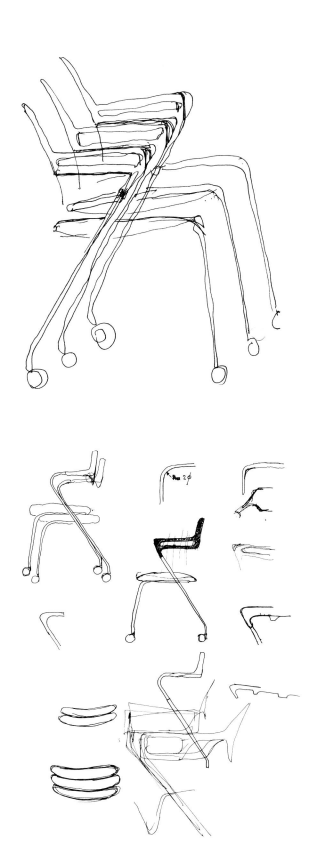

TONIX

Office furniture systems, Vitra

1992, Spatio, with Glen Oliver Löw;
1994, Ad Hoc, with Glen Oliver Löw;
1996, Monowall, with Glen Oliver Löw;
2000, Vademecum, with Glen Oliver Löw;
2001, Ad Wall, Transphere

"In the office sector being an architect is very important," says Citterio: "only through study of the layout is it possible to understand exactly what the needs of users are. We were among the first to think that the worktable did not have to be a regular table. We began to talk about flexibility and developed products out of this concept. Knowing how an office functions, it is possible to design objects that solve the problems."
The office furniture he has developed with Vitra responds well to the now rapid and continual changes in the workplace, and in the way we work in general.

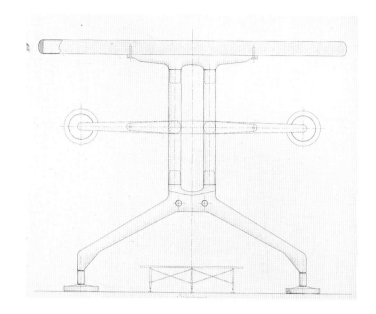

SPATIO

SPATIO

SPATIO

Ever since Spatio in 1992 his collaboration with Vitra on systems of furniture has been oriented toward the construction of models that can be adapted to different situations and with a strong reference to languages and contexts outside the specific tradition of products for the office. Tables, chests of drawers and bookcases, made out of natural wood on structures of aluminum and steel, hold an explicit dialogue with the characteristics of household furniture. They employ solutions that make it easy to move and arrange the furniture in space. Cleanliness of overall design and clarity of construction and in the use of the materials distinguish Spatio, which went in an original direction in the panorama of the office at the beginning of the nineties.

He went further down the road of flexibility of organization and location in space in 1994 with Ad Hoc, whose name already reflects the desire to respond to precise needs. And that is how it was in fact presented: "Team office, non-territorial office, desk sharing, lean office, combi office, home office: these are the scenarios for the future of the office. Mobility is the new watchword, to work anywhere and at any time, to be able to communicate as well as concentrate. All these conditions characterize Ad Hoc." Furniture—such as movable tables combined with partitions, chests of drawers and small containers fitted with big handles to make them easy to move—that permits different arrangements for individual work, for conversation, for meetings. Over time this system was integrated with Monowall, Vademecum, Ad Wall and Transphere (forming a comprehensive range known as Ad Office), providing variable configurations of tables, new partitions and units designed to hold electronic devices and even offering complete plans for workplaces to meet specific requirements. The system has a number of distinctive stylistic elements, from cunning combinations of color between the white worktops and the bright hues of the storage units (something not very common in the sector and capable of giving them a familiar and relaxed appearance) and partitions with large and regular holes to the overall simplification in the composition of individual objects. A simplification that is clearly connected with the necessities and characteristics of industrial production.

AD HOC

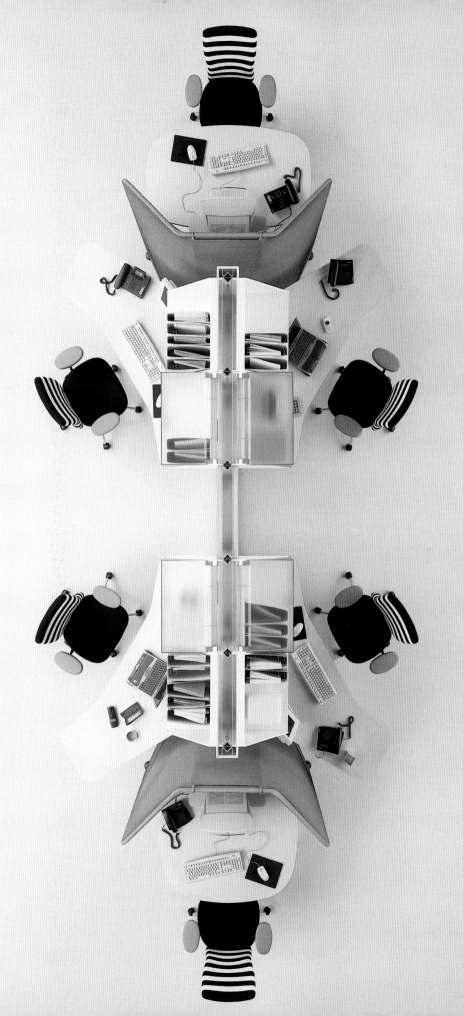

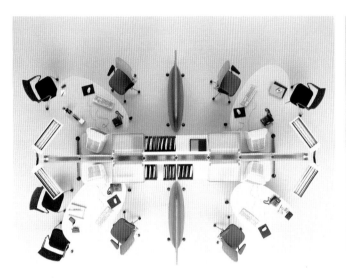

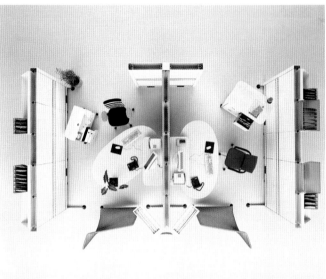

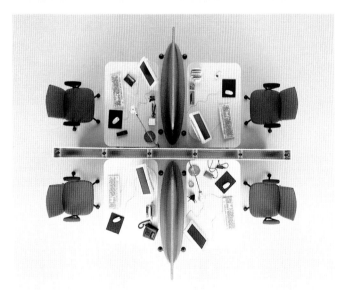

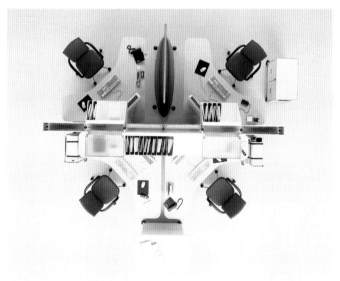

AD WALL

MONOWALL

VADEMECUM

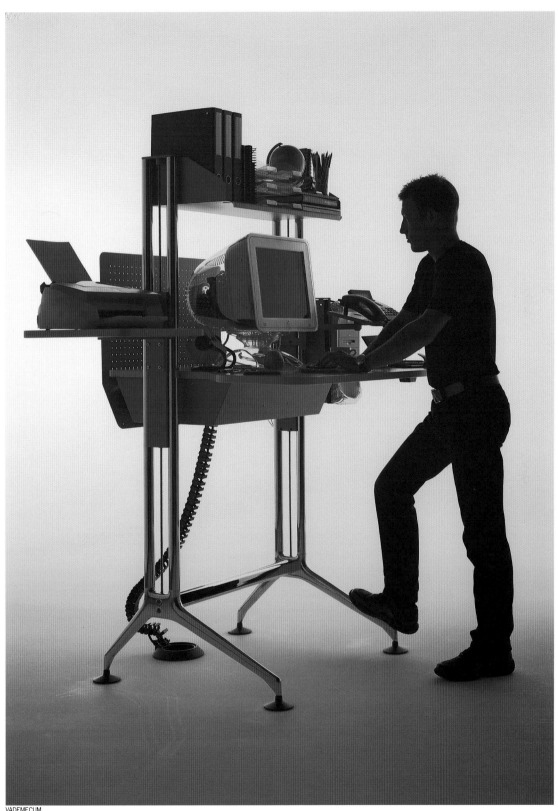

TRANSPHERE

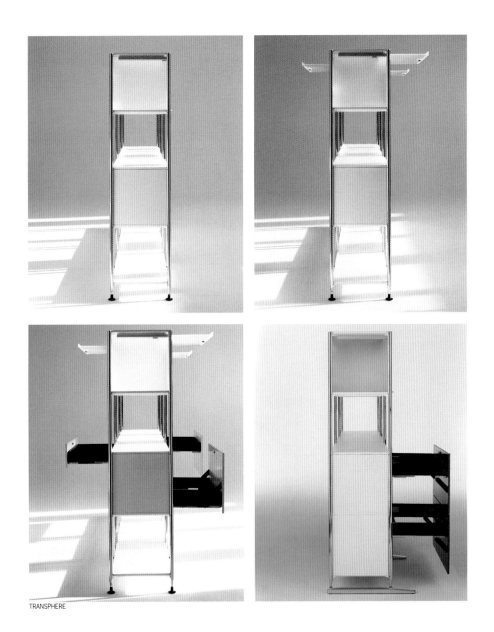

TRANSPHERE

Lighting systems, Ansorg

1993, Elettra, with Glen Oliver Löw; 1994,
Quadra (Ansorg/Belux), with Glen Oliver Löw;
1996, Camera, with Glen Oliver Löw; 1998,
Alumina, with Glen Oliver Löw; 2002, Brick,
with Glen Oliver Löw

The study of the Ansorg lighting systems was
carried out in relation to particular areas of use,
especially those of sales outlets and workplaces.
Ansorg is a subsidiary of the Vitra group and
the design of the lamps was connected with
the Vitrashop-Visplay range for retail stores and office systems. Active in both sectors, Citterio has
developed a close dialogue between the design of
furniture and of dedicated lighting systems. Elettra
constituted his first venture into the field of lamps,
as well as providing an example of the designer's
ability to handle and give shape to precise requirements of performance and function.
Elettra is distinguished by its ability to create a
focus point: the beam of light can be easily and
precisely oriented by moving a handle. The lamp
is adjusted and blocked in place by means of a
small lever, derived from the bicycle sector. Thus
the solution, at once anonymous and familiar, has
been borrowed from other fields of design and
goes hand in hand with the adoption of technical
materials and mechanisms in the manufacturing
process and to determine the characteristics of
the light. The mode of operation is revealed and
"domesticated" by the presence of the handle,
but the whole thing is couched in a homogeneous
and predominantly technical language.
Another element of the approach to the sector
is its systemic character, in which the design
focuses not on a single piece of equipment, but

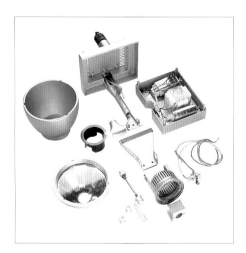

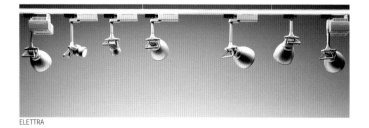

ELETTRA

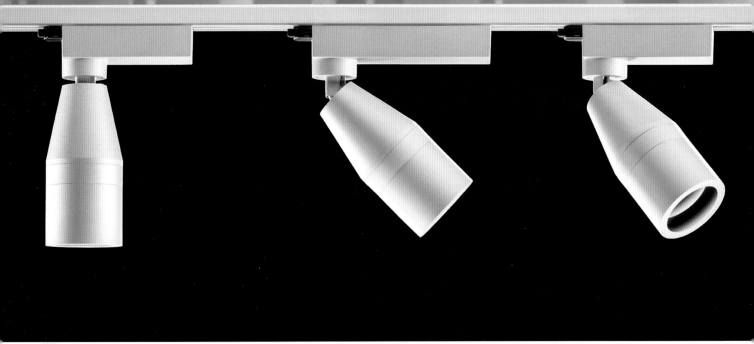

BRICK

on a set of connected elements capable of meeting a range of needs, in this case pertaining to the illumination of a sales outlet.

A similar logic of design has been applied to the Camera spotlight, which is visually and functionally reminiscent of photographic equipment in its form as well as in the mechanism that is used to adjust the size and direction of the beam of light. The lamp is constructed principally from two materials that respond to different requirements: the natural anodized aluminum of the internal casing acts as a heat sink, while the plastic outer casing allows the light to be gripped and adjusted. A spot mounted on the ceiling, or on a stand, and equipped with profiling lenses, filters and focusing device, it projects a beam of light that can be adjusted by means of an articulated joint.

Quadra, on the other hand, is intended chiefly for workspaces: combining direct light for the individual workstation and indirect light for the surroundings, it provides an effective solution to problems of illumination and is able to cope with real operating needs. It is available in floor, table and wall versions, and permits the insertion of screens and colored diffusers. Developed over time specifically for use in connection with Vitra's Ad Hoc office system and then produced by the Belux lighting company, it found an appropriate use when computers came into widespread use. In fact the introduction of the computer has profoundly modified lighting requirements, demanding responses that are at once precise, like that of a desk lamp with characteristics suited to the use of the monitor, and versatile in order to cope with variations in the organization of the working methods, functions and hours. The design of Quadra is distinguished by the geometric casing that contains the light sources and the elegant Y-shaped support.

While Quadra is characterized by its square form, Alumina is hemispherical, soft and rounded. The floor model reinterprets the Luminator model with its indirect lighting through the adoption of a sophisticated material like aluminum and clean lines, based on the asymmetry between the diffuser in the form of an upturned bowl and the stand. Alumina fully represents Citterio's approach to lighting: it resolves questions of technique, function and performance while handling them in a language that reflects current developments in design.

QUADRA

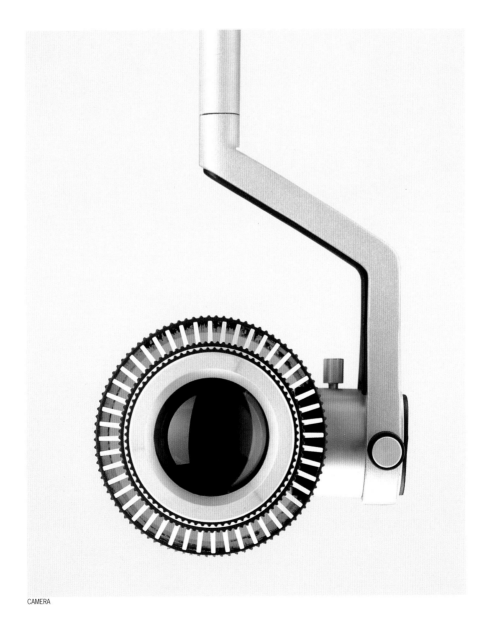

CAMERA

Trolleys, folding tables and mobile storage units, Kartell

1991, Battista trolley-table, Leopoldo
trolley-table, Gastone trolley-table, Oxo trolley,
with Glen Oliver Löw;
1994, Mobil storage unit, with Glen Oliver Löw

"When I got married in 1989 I looked for a trolley and could find nothing interesting on the
market. So I designed one," Citterio recalls.
Born out of personal need, this project went on
to achieve great commercial success and critical recognition.
"Unlike with other companies, Citterio works with
Kartell," declares its proprietor Claudio Luti, "on
the design of an individual piece or series of
pieces. The trolleys, which were the first objects
we produced together, entailed a long period of
research. After more than a year we were still
not satisfied and decided to start again from the
beginning. I was impressed by the honesty of
the designer, who chose to start again from
scratch rather than stick with a product that he
did not find fully convincing. And then Citterio
quickly came up with the right idea."
Battista, Leopoldo and Gastone make up a
range of trolleys and folding tables that are
characterized in the first place by the combination of steel, aluminum and plastic. They offer
several new solutions and design features: the
extending mechanism, which has been derived
from the tradition of anonymous design; the
slender design of the legs, which recalls the
lines of Eames's chairs; the plastic top in various

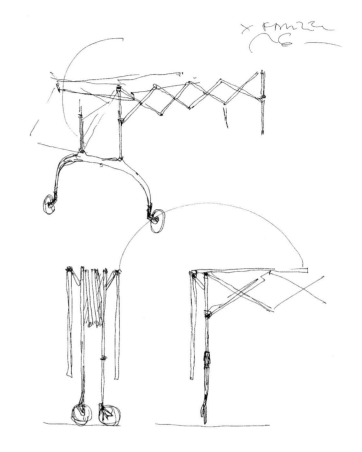

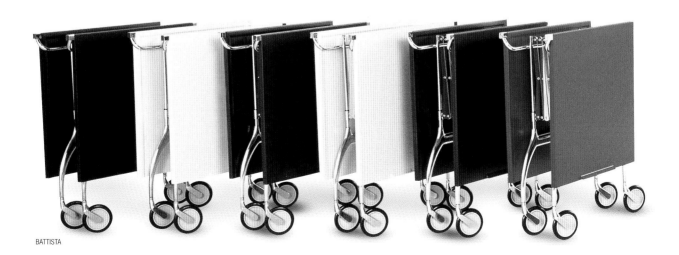

BATTISTA

colors, clean and essential but given a "domestic" appearance by the treatment of the surface; and finally the unusual wheels, used for the entire series of Kartell objects, which were to inspire many similar versions. Overall, they are products whose design has been completely reassessed, but which have an extremely familiar look, as they are rooted in our shared memories of this type of object.

An analogous alphabet of signs, commencing with the wheels, which in this case are paired and fitted with brakes, has been adopted for the multifunctional Oxo trolleys (the name derives from the X-shaped piece of die-cast aluminum that confers stability on the structure), providing an ideal solution for the support of a computer or television.

In both cases a thorough study of the design of the parts has been carried out in relation to technical and manufacturing requirements, with regard to the plastic materials and the metals.

It was observation of the characteristics and effect of sandblasted glass that inspired the research into sandblasted plastic, which was adopted for the first time in the Mobil storage units. The method used to produce the material, a system of injection molding for which special studies were carried out, is extremely interesting. In this Citterio was able to count on the solid and extensive experience of the Kartell company. Founded after the war by Giulio Castelli, it has specialized in the development and production of plastic materials, coupled with the design of furniture and

BATTISTA AND GASTONE

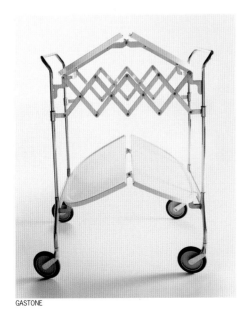
GASTONE

LEOPOLDO

household objects. The latter is an aspect that has been further expanded since the nineties, under the guidance of Claudio Luti, through collaborations with major international designers. "Fundamental for this product," says Luti, "was the work of reducing the elements to a minimum, a sort of destructuring of the object, and again the union of a new plastic with the light metal structure. Mobil remains one of our bestselling pieces as well as being highly visible and recognizable."

The result achieved with Mobil represents an important contribution to the revival of the whole sector, having made it possible to get over the rather cheap connotation of ordinary opaque plastic and to design products with a special type of value, derived entirely from the treatment of the surfaces and the tactile and visual characteristics. The Mobil trolleys—awarded the Compasso d'Oro in 1994—retain some of the features of the earlier collections, such as the wheels and the slender steel tubing that makes up the supporting framework but also contains the slides for insertion of the drawers.

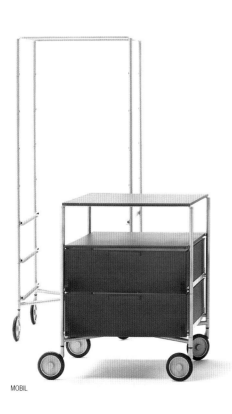

MOBIL

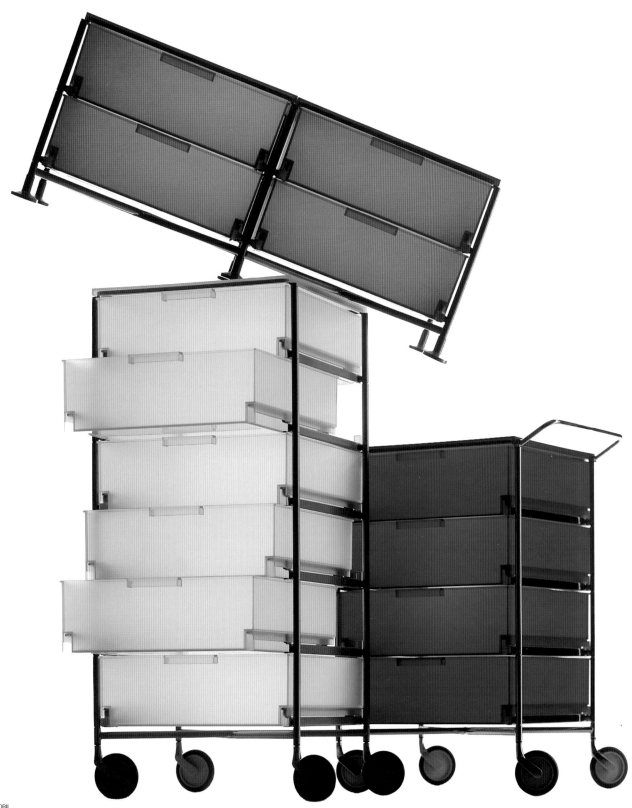

MOBIL

111

OXO

OXO

OXO

113

Emme system of hospital furniture
Industrie Guido Malvestio
with Stefano Gallizioli

The opportunity to carry out research into hospital furniture for the Paduan company Malvestio was provided by a competition staged by the French Ministry of Health to develop new standards of quality for hospital beds. Citterio's design work was preceded by a long phase of preparation and consultation with doctors and nurses, essential to a thorough understanding of the problems involved in their utilization. One of the central questions to emerge was the need to be able to carry out certain types of operations around the bed, such as sterilizing objects. This made it necessary to conduct extensive research into the appropriate structural solutions, the materials to be adopted and the most effective structural details. The system is made entirely from die-cast aluminum parts (although some of these were later to be replaced by plastic components), assembled without the use of screws. Color was also introduced, something fairly unusual for the sector. The use of aluminum responds to the requirements of structural reliability, lightness and resistance to washing and corrosion. In the same way, the plastic materials are able to guarantee

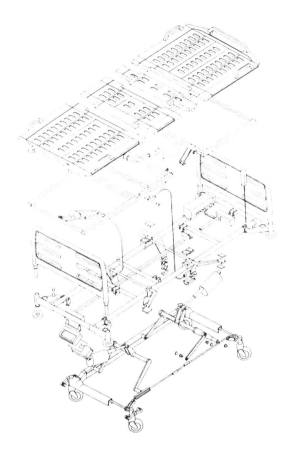

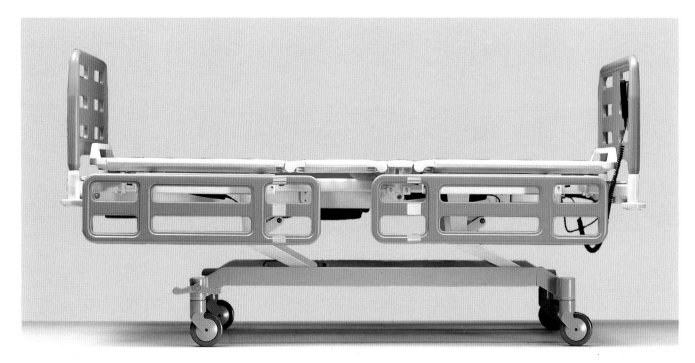

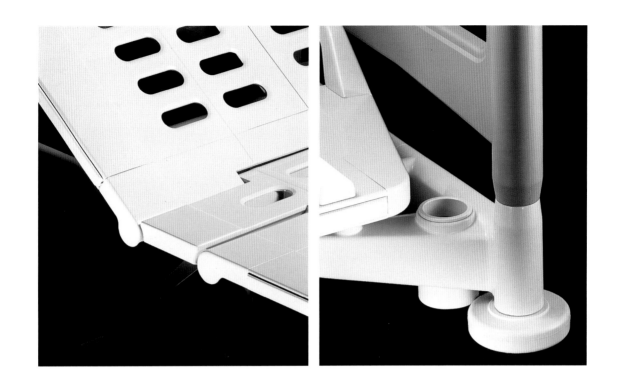

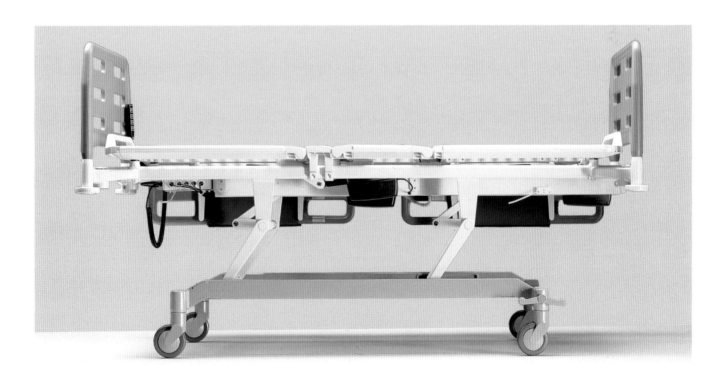

a degree of resistance to chemical agents and fire and make it possible to produce light but strong parts thanks to the technique of single-block double-shell molding. On the basis of these choices, the company has developed a new system of production for the assembly of composite materials that has required various investments in technology, including systems for automated welding, laser cutting and molding of the components, as well as permitting the elimination of visible welds and the integration of the mechanical pieces into the structural elements. In addition, specific attention has been paid to the environmental sustainability of both the product and the manufacturing process: the pieces are made of a single, individually identified material, easy to dismantle and recycle. The finishing of the surfaces with epoxy-polyester powders makes it possible to avoid using galvanic treatments, with their associated emission of polluting substances.

The work of design has been extended to embrace the whole range of hospital furniture, including tables, bedside tables and armchairs. The system stands out for its unusual area of application, to which the architect has been able to bring the know-how derived from his experience in the furniture sector. The interest in ergonomic aspects and technical and functional requirements, the care taken over engineering and structural solutions and the effort to reduce the impact on the environment represent some of the many elements of a design that is of high quality, in an aesthetically attractive style, and above all one that perfectly answers the needs.

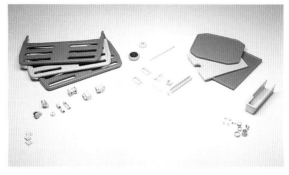

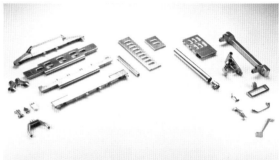

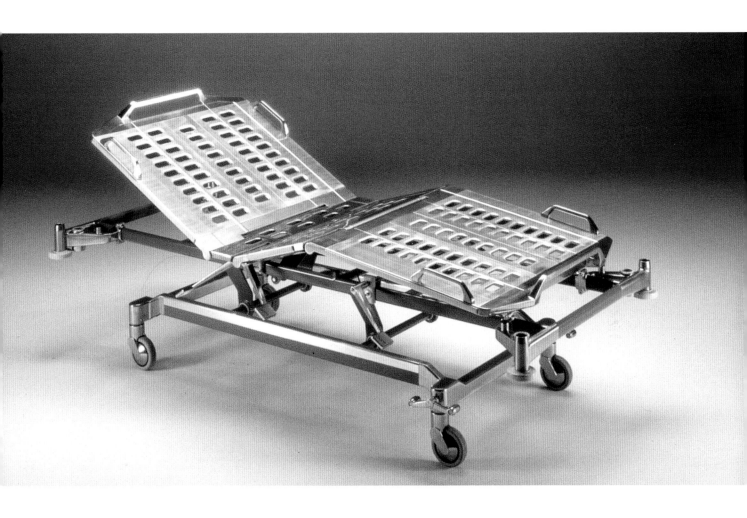

Compagnia delle Filippine armchairs and seats
B&B Italia

"The interest of this collection," argues Citterio, "lies in the fact that, at the beginning of the nineties, it raised a question that has since become highly topical, that of the delocalization of manufacturing and its related problems, commencing with production costs. However paradoxical it might seem, sometimes the handmade product costs less than the industrial one."
The collection of seats for the company (a division of B&B Italia set up in the seventies) is made out of rattan (a type of climbing palm characterized by its density, thickness and uniformity) on the island of Mindanao, in the Philippines. For the designer this meant carrying out a careful study of the material and its structural possibilities and modes of production. As far as this last aspect is concerned, the difficulties of applying the logic of standardization typical of industry are obvious and it is necessary instead for the design process to take into account the specific nature of the local model of production. Out of the designer's intention to combine the traditional material with soft and rounded forms, set on slender legs, came seats with two types of plaited covering, in rattan or thin strips of buffalo leather in natural colors. The concealed padding is in polyurethane, while the structure and the legs are made of wood and terminate in aluminum feet.

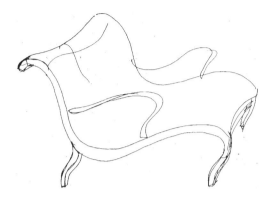

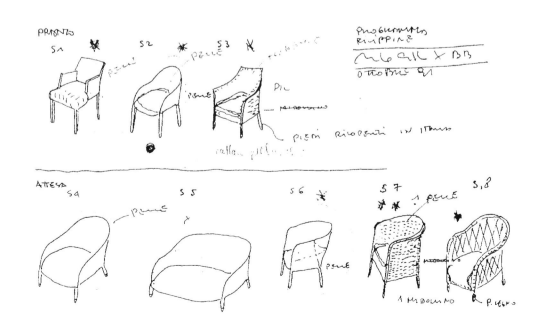

Door handles, Fusital

1995, AC1 Novantacinque,
AC2 Novantacinque;
2000, K2;
2003, AC3, with Toan Nguyen

"My work in the sector of door handles," declares Citterio, "consists in redesigning classical models by studying small details and new proportions that become their distinctive elements." The architect, who began to collaborate with Fusital in the early nineties, chose to contribute to the company's general production with objects of deliberately muted character, whose recognizability stems from the detail. In this choice Citterio remained faithful to his approach to design: "The care of the detail is the product." In this case the details consist of the treatment of the finish and the design of the collar or neck. Citterio adds: "I really enjoy designing these small objects. They are prehensile, minimal, metal, dry, precise. Moreover, the automated production of door handles means that it is necessary to construct the form in relation to the manufacturing procedures, whether you are working with metal tubing or casting."
The pair of door handles designed in 1995, reconsiderations of archetypal and anonymous forms and given rounded shapes that are easy to grip, was followed by another series in 2000, more geometric in style but enriched by the contrast between the smooth and satin finishes of the steel.

AC1 NOVANTACINQUE

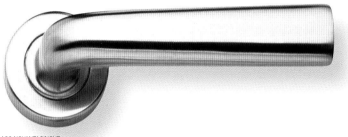

AC2 NOVANTACINQUE

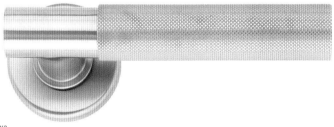

K2

120

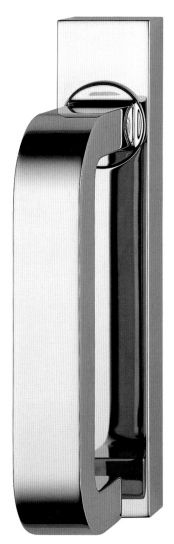

AC3

System of sofas, B&B Italia

1995, Harry; 1998, Charles

"In those years I was working on the interior design of a private house," recalls Citterio, "and wanted a sofa with a suspended structure on which to place cushions. Harry was born out of this necessity and I was certainly also inspired by the memory of some of Florence Knoll's sofas from the sixties, which handled the overall form in a sophisticated way by basing it visually on the corner." The stylistic formula of the supporting structure set on slender legs re-proposed by the design of Harry, in contrast with common models that stand on the ground, became a benchmark for much of the production in the second half of the nineties. Thus Harry is characterized by its rigorous supporting structure (a framework of steel tubing and sections, filled with cold-foamed polyurethane and upholstered) on which are laid the cushions, a system the architect had been adopting ever since Diesis; the presence of short legs in shiny brushed aluminum, terminating in cones to which the feet are fixed with screws; the visual emphasis placed on the edges; the deep and comfortable seat. The complete system is made up of sofas in three lengths, an armchair and a number of modular elements, including a terminal chaise-longue, interesting because it anticipates the island structure developed in the subsequent Charles. "Charles, which has been a great commercial success as well as being much imitated," declares the designer, "is one of my

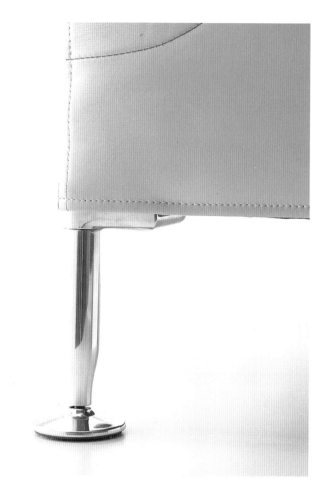

HARRY

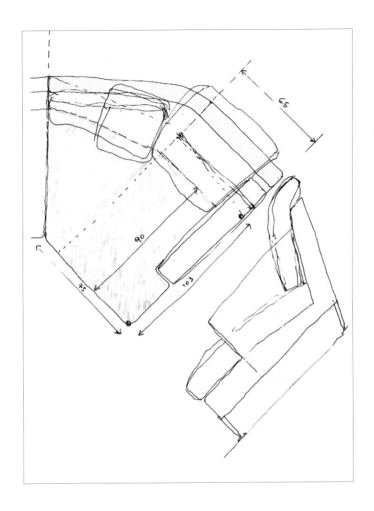

HARRY

best pieces, both for the simplicity of its structure and line and for its re-proposal of the idea of the island sofa, achieved by the organic integration of the chaise-longue." An intuition that clearly originated with Sity, but that has been reinterpreted in this model in a reductionist language. The linear structure of the sofa is softened by the slight internal splaying of the arm-back, accentuated by contrast with the characteristic three-way leg set on the corner; it also has a free part that functions as a light end piece. "The apparently simple and easy design of my sofas," he continues, "is the result of a familiarity with the technique of construction and production refined over the years. While I design all the details relating to my objects analytically, in a way I 'recount' the sofas, in the sense that it is sufficient for me to make a precise description of what I have in mind for the ideas then, in collaboration with the B&B Research and Development Center, to be turned into a product. For sofas the cut of the fabric is also important; to some extent I work like a tailor who starts out from the cutting of the material when he constructs a suit." Charles offers the possibility of composing a large number of seats out of sixteen elements; a single cushion-seat with a series of free cushions resting against the back, also available in davenport and bed versions, completed by low tables, all with the same legs made of shiny brushed aluminum, and used to construct a versatile and homogeneous system that can be used anywhere in the home.

CHARLES

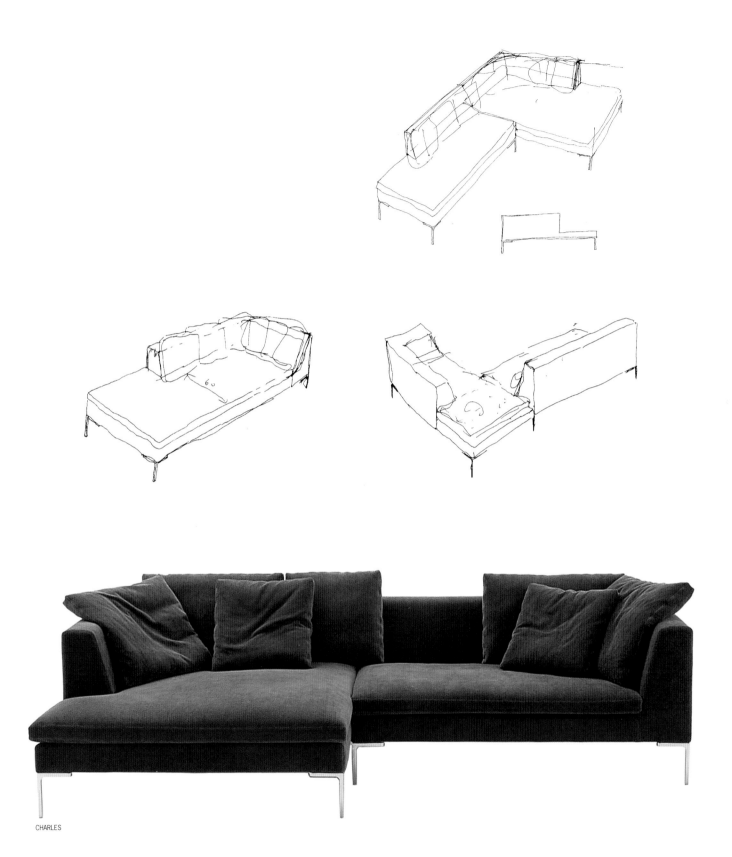

CHARLES

Collection of furnishings, Maxalto-B&B Italia

1996, Apta; 2003, AC Collection

For the Maxalto brand (a member of the B&B Italia group since the end of the seventies) Citterio works on classical typologies for furnishing the rooms of the house. A different approach with respect to his products for B&B, conceived on the whole for a fluid space, not constrained by precise limitations of dimension and divisions. Citterio tackled the project for Maxalto from the perspective of interior rather than industrial design, partly in view of the characteristics of the company's production, much of it of a hand-crafted type.

It is a complete range of furniture intended to meet the needs of a domestic setting with precise spatial limitations: furnishings constructed in terms of volumes and masses, characterized by the use of fine materials and simple in design and execution, that keep the distinctive and recognizable sign to a minimum. The first collection for Maxalto took its inspiration from the tradition of the interior decoration of the 1920s, with imposing sofas and objects made of dark wood with hard and angular lines, combined with details in steel for tables and cabinets.

Later ranges like Apta interpret the theme of furnishing with greater freedom and invention, using paler wood, fabrics in neutral tones and softer and more graceful lines.

"In a single object design is able to reach a conclusion," says Citterio, "but it is very difficult to work on systems. The Maxalto collections apply the logic of the single piece to the construction of a complete suite of furniture." And again: "I believe that the design of a piece of furniture consists in creating a setting in which the object, through its use, its position, its relationship with the other objects, participates in a ritual of domestic components. Rituality represents the essence of the bourgeois culture of the house."

So Citterio works by individual "pieces" that redesign typologies, such as the *étagère*, or containers for meals or the buffet, which are cleaned up by freeing them of decorative frills and rendered essential and functional instead.

APTA

AC COLLECTION

1996

Dolly chair
Kartell
with Glen Oliver Löw

Dolly encapsulates several interesting design themes. On the one hand the presence of the arms makes it comfortable to use but also stackable; on the other it can be folded by means of a simple hinge mechanism concealed in the leg. Thanks to this device it has an overall configuration that, in addition to rendering the supporting structure (legs-arms-back) continuous, gives it a somewhat organic appearance, particularly evident in the unusual curve of the arms, connected to the back in a single piece. A stylistic choice that is not very common in Citterio's work, but which recalls similar solutions in his seats for Vitra or the Spoon stool for Kartell and answers perfectly to the functional and structural requirements of the product.

A distinctive feature is the use of a new plastic—bulk-colored polypropylene, extended with minerals and glass fiber—that allows different thicknesses to be produced while avoiding shrinkage of the material. This has made it possible to obtain sealed surfaces of a quality comparable to those of aluminum and die-cast metals. Specific research has been carried out into the coloring and the seats, proposed in several materials and finishes, plastic as well as wood, making Dolly suitable for use in different settings.

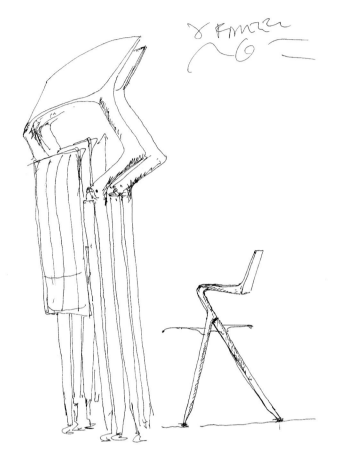

PROTOTYPE

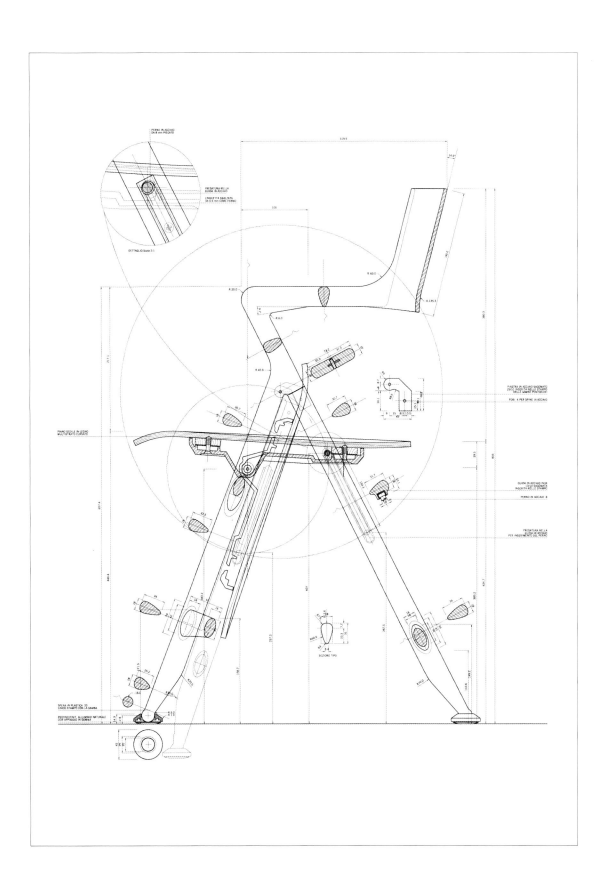

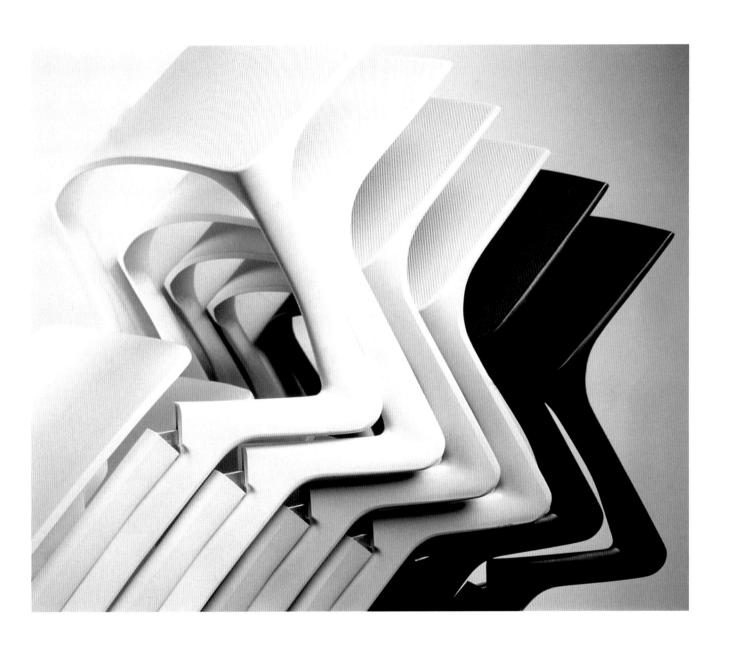

Minni chair
Halifax-Tisettanta

Minni is a stackable seat with or without arms, the outcome of a reflection on classic models like the Thonet chairs, redesigned to suit contemporary production technologies and materials.

On the subject of this object produced by Halifax (a brand of the Tisettanta group), Citterio declares: "I spurn an excess of signs, invention for its own sake." The solutions adopted in Minni are a perfect illustration of these principles. Its distinctive feature is the structural seat made of polyamide reinforced with glass fiber, its thickness differentiated to cope with variations in load, to which the various components of the chair are fixed: legs and arms in solid beech or natural anodized aluminum, seat and back in polypropylene lightened by circular openings, padded and upholstered if required. It is an advanced design from the viewpoint of the industrialization of the manufacturing process, which finds expression in a very simple language yet one that is eloquent in its overall effect and in its juxtaposition of materials.

In addition to the avowed reference to nineteenth-century Viennese chairs, it is possible to discern more than one allusion to the tradition of design, from Philippe Starck's model with a similar coupling of wood and plastic to Enzo Mari's chair with a perforated seat. It is a testimony to his effort to understand the archetypes, a mark of his vision of design as a continual process of improvement of the product.

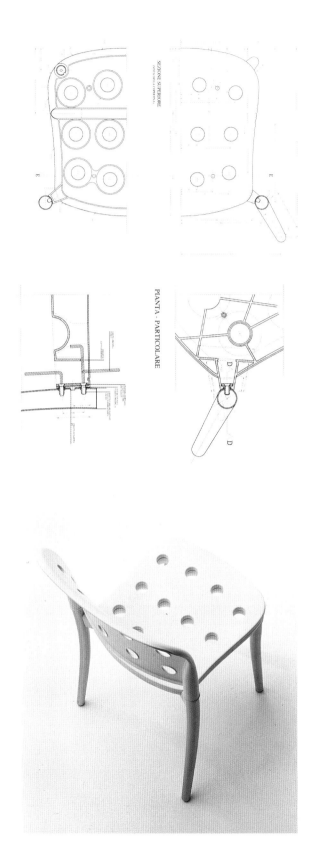

Flatware and utensils

1996/2003, Sawaya&Moroni/Guzzini;
1998, 2000, Hackman-Iittala,
with Glen Oliver Löw

The theme of flatware for the table and utensils for the kitchen has a very old tradition and it is one that Citterio has frequently tried his hand at. The service designed for Sawaya&Moroni was inspired, he recalls, by the model produced in the forties by Luigi Caccia Dominioni, resulting in slender and elongated flatware of graceful form, made out of silver. Left at the prototype stage, the set has recently been adapted by Guzzini for mass production in stainless steel.
The collaboration with Hackman-Iittala was of a different character. The Finnish company has a historic manufacturing plant specializing in the working of steel where studies have been launched into the design and production of sets of flatware (Citterio 1998, Citterio 2000), kitchen knives and implements (Citterio Collective Tools and Toolbox). The point of departure for the research was the technology at the company's disposal, in particular a pressed material of reduced thickness chosen for the flatware, which made it possible to work on the tactile character of the surface. For the knives on the other hand a special technique for welding steel bars has been adopted that makes the object look seamless, without any sign of a join between handle and blade. The architect has carried out specific research into the ergonomic aspect, the correct way of gripping and utilizing flatware and utensils, which has conditioned the dimensions, the design of the curves and the balancing of the weights.

IITTALA

134

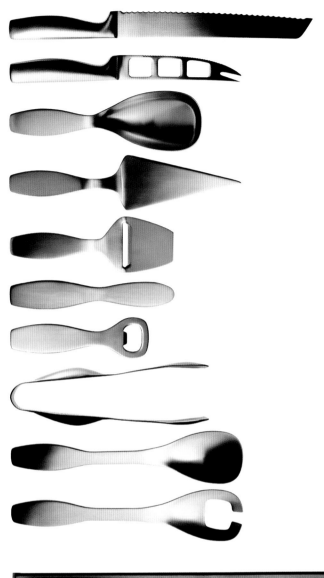

IITTALA

IITTALA

SAWAYA&MORONI/GUZZINI

Artist computer
Max Data
with Glen Oliver Löw

The collaboration with the German company Max Data has given Citterio an opportunity to tackle products based on complex technology, with results that are interesting from the viewpoint of method and of the possibility of transferring know-how and understanding derived from other spheres to specialized sectors. In fact opportunities like this are not seized very often and the design of such objects remains the prerogative of "specialists" who are technically skilled but do not always give priority to the aspects of interface and use and to the overall quality of the product in general. It is a question to which greater attention has been paid in recent years, but which was not yet considered crucial in the middle of the nineties, when Citterio worked for Max Data. A characteristic element of the mini-tower models is the underlining of the pillar structure, which emphasizes the reference to the architectural member with a "foot" along the sides of the base, which also helps to make it stable. Similarly, the tabletop versions have square and rational forms with measured modeling of light and shade. A specific program of research was conducted into the design of the interface of the parts at the front, especially the buttons, as well as the surface textures and colors, which led to the adoption of a sober but fairly unusual shade of pale gray.

System of doors, Tre Più

1998, Pavilion; 1999, Planus

The research carried out for Tre Più and the products that have stemmed from it are based on the idea of coming up with a really industrialized solution for the production of components for interiors, with regard both to the individual elements (doors, windows, movable partitions and sliding doors) and their installation. The contribution requested from the designer was to solve this problem in an efficient, inexpensive and aesthetically attractive way. Starting out from the personal experience of designing the doors of his own studio and house and having them made by hand, Citterio went on to investigate the possibilities of engineering manual processes of construction to make them applicable on an industrial scale, so that they could be used for real mass production. This research into the mechanisms of operation, construction and installation of doors and partitions is continuing, for the same company, in an attempt to come up with similar solutions for outdoor components and doors and windows.

In short, the Pavilion sliding doors are intended to be "a project for the design of space," inasmuch as the system frees it from the rigidity and opacity of walls and divides it up instead with light and dynamic structures, proposed as an "architectural" element of furnishing.

The distinctive feature of the Planus doors, on the other hand, is the way they close flush with the wall, making it easy to integrate them into the setting. The technical and structural solutions, like the patented hinges whose height and depth can be adjusted and the aluminum jambs, are very carefully thought out.

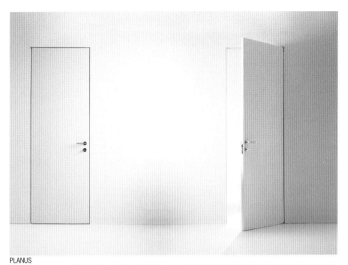

PLANUS

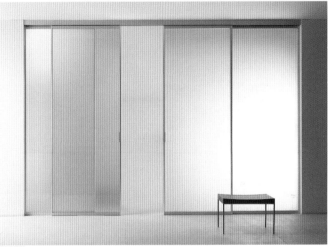

PAVILION

1998

ABC system of seats
Flexform

The ABC system of seats harks back to the rationalist style of the 1930s (as did the work he had previously carried out for Flexform) in its use of black leather and of continuous lengths of metal tubing for legs and arms. However, the idea of the very low-slung seat, at floor level, is a strictly contemporary one and serves to integrate the volumes of the large square cushions into the nearly cubic form circumscribed by the structure of chromed or satin metal tubing.

It is certainly the redesign of an object from the past, but one into which he has also introduced a sophisticated patented mechanism for tilting the back and making the seat comfortable.

There are several ways in which a product like ABC is an indication of Citterio's constant reflection on the tradition of industrial design, and at the same time of his ability to update it, in style and function, in line with the manufacturer's modes of production. In fact the collaboration with Flexform has allowed him to explore simple and essential solutions that are related to a handcrafted and accurate approach to the process of construction.

Lastra hanging lamp
Flos
with Glen Oliver Löw

Lastra constitutes a stimulating reflection on familiar functional typologies of the past, such as the lamp to be hung above a table, redesigned in the light of changing visual sensibilities and the potentialities of new technology. For this design Citterio has chosen a simple sheet of glass (a material that conjures up images of the chandelier) which uses remote-controlled halogen light sources and has the electronic circuits for adjusting their brightness printed directly onto the surface. "A lamp," explains Enrico Morteo, "but above all a spatial system, a piece of stage equipment that works on the naked structure of light." Lastra is a hanging lamp that produces direct light, with a body of transparent tempered glass and, depending on the model, either six or eight diffusers made of pressed glass and painted white. The starting point for the design was his observation of the printed circuit of the heated rear window of an automobile, which determined his choice of the system for the transmission of electricity. In fact this is supplied to the light sources through two distinct processes of silkscreen printing: a highly conductive silver paste is deposited during the first passage, and then this is covered with a protective ceramic-based varnish on the second. The lamp is suspended from the ceiling by four steel wires. A light and transparent presence in space that exposes its technical innards "to view," the lamp is an example of his attention to the interaction between design and technology, undoubtedly one of today's central themes. The project also marked the beginning of Citterio's collaboration with the Brescian company Flos, one of the most important lighting manufacturers in the world and the producer of Achille and Pier Giacomo Castiglioni's models, among others. Founded in 1962 and run for a long time by Sergio Gandini, Flos has been vigorously expanded by his son Piero over the last two decades. "Lastra is at once a technological object and a household article," says Citterio, "that started out from an effort to solve a problem, that of providing direct lighting of the place setting, rather than from a research into form." And he goes on: "Of course the best lighting for a dinner table comes from candles, whose play of light and shade is highly atmospheric. In a way Lastra sets out to create an ambience of this kind. It is a technological object, a piece of stage machinery that functions like a lighting director's control room, but which had its origin in an emotional concept."

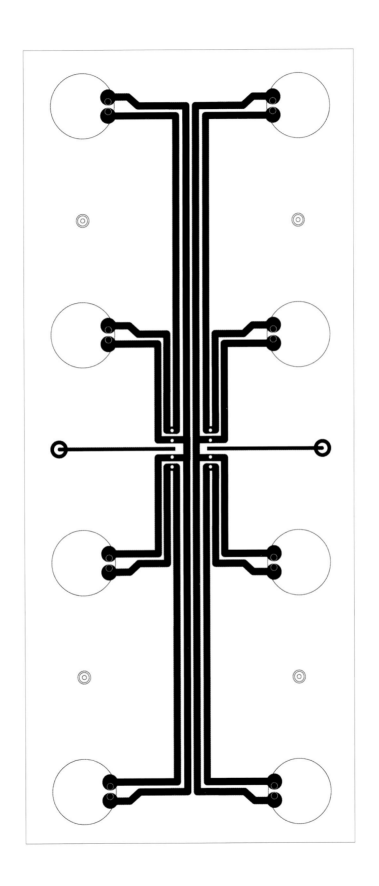

Concept and research for television sets, Brionvega
with Toan Nguyen

One of the major themes of contemporary design is the design of technological objects. Citterio was given an interesting opportunity to work in this field by the research he carried out for Brionvega. A historic Italian company founded by the enterprising businessman Ennio Brion, it has collaborated with, among others, Marco Zanuso and Richard Sapper, Achille and Pier Giacomo Castiglioni and Mario Bellini, producing objects that have become part of the history of contemporary design. In 1998 the Brionvega brand was acquired by the Formenti group, which has faced the difficult task of continuing a demanding tradition of quality design, in a context where research and technology have grown increasingly decisive.

Citterio's collaboration with Brionvega did not reach the production phase, but has indicated numerous possible directions in which the design of television sets can be taken. In close relation

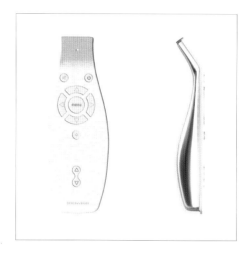

to the technological means adopted in each case, some of the designs present a more traditional appearance, while others are more innovative and reflect the developments in the sector. An example of this is the theme of the dematerialization of the television set, of an appliance without a frame, investigated by Citterio through the use of flat screens (plasma technology was just coming into widespread use at the time) and large sheets of glass mounted on the wall on which to print, for instance, the circuits of the speakers. An important reference for the work has been the comparison with the conceptual and structural logic of the computer, based on the progressive implementation of technical and functional elements and features. Taking this criterion as a starting point, he designed models with a screen set on a linear stand of metal tubing that also serves as a support for the geometric housing of the electronic components.

They are objects couched in a contemporary language and blend easily into the contemporary home or workplace, partly because they share a common and correct approach to design.

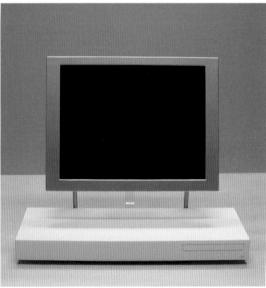

1999

Freetime system of sofas
B&B Italia

The fundamental characteristic of Freetime is its use of solid metal tubing with very tight angles of curvature, producing an effect of considerable elegance, refinement and quality of construction. A choice that is reminiscent of the furniture of the thirties, and the armchairs of Le Corbusier in particular, and that makes other allusions to that period, such as the models of Mies van der Rohe, above all his couch with a back that could be adjusted to different heights.

The adoption of solid metal tubing entailed a specific study of the connecting elements, for which a solution was found that was at once effective and rational from the viewpoint of production.

More in general, it is a metal framework on which large square cushions are set, in accordance with Citterio's now classic formula of separation of the supported and supporting parts. Freetime is a flexible system that permits different spatial configurations based on various arrangements of the individual elements: it can be used to create comfortable sofas and armchairs with metal arms, to organize the seats in space, with islands or adjustable chaiseslongues, or again to "free" the tubing of the back, using it simply as a support for cushions. A distinctive feature of the design is the use of visible bands to connect and support the structure and seat.

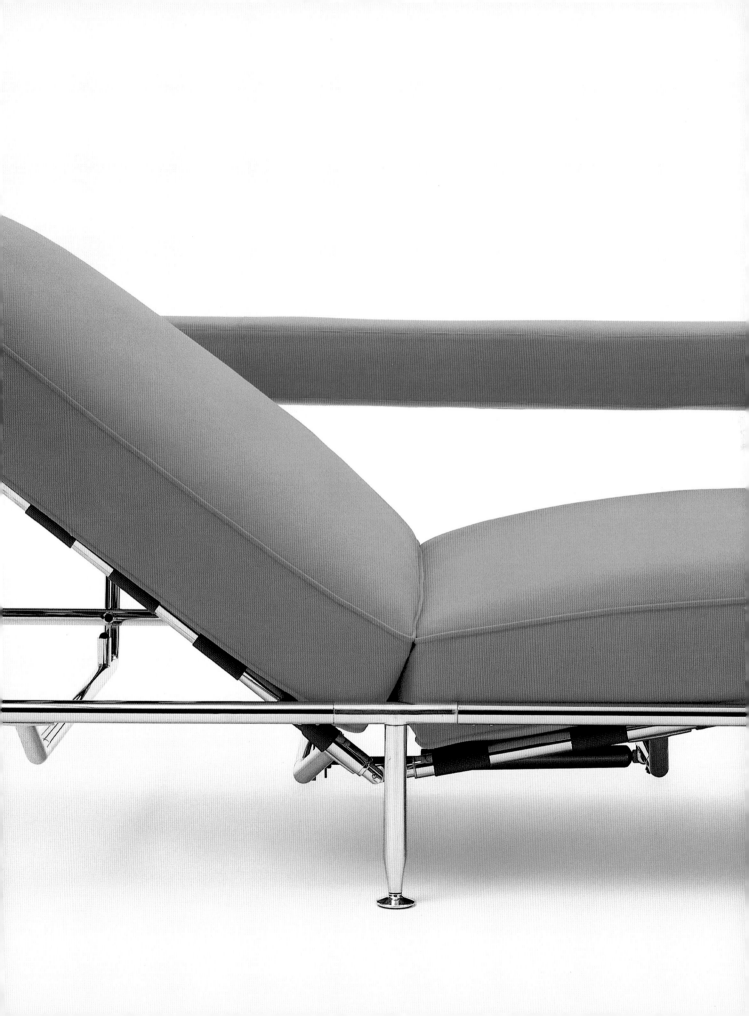

Bathroom fittings

1999, H₂0, Inda, with Sergio Brioschi;
2000, 500, Join, Pozzi Ginori,
with Sergio Brioschi;
2003, Easy, Q³, Pozzi Ginori,
with Sergio Brioschi

Toward the end of the nineties Citterio began to devote his attention to themes linked to the bathroom, designing products and concepts. The objects he conceived and designed for two different companies in the sector, Inda and Pozzi Ginori, have a number of elements in common. With Inda he set out to exploit the company's production capacities linked to the use of metal, and steel tubing in particular. The H₂0 collection is made up of containers, washbasins, shower cabins and accessories, capable of providing a complete set of fittings. Worthy of particular attention is the Frame series, for which the designer has arranged small fittings, all the classic bathroom accessories, around structures of steel tubing sometimes combined with surfaces of colored or transparent plastic with a satin finish, or equipped with slides for mirrors, shelves and doors. The objective of extending the theme of design from individual pieces to complete layouts for the bathroom has been taken further with Pozzi Ginori, a historic Italian manufacturer specializing in ceramic sanitary fixtures. At the base of the design of the products lies the idea of creating washbasins with ample surfaces on which to place objects, while addressing particular attention to reducing their overall size, so that they can fit easily into small spaces. The washbasins and sanitary fixtures are characterized by the mixtilinear forms of the wall mountings and the surfaces. These choices are intended to appeal to a wide range of customers through their use of a functional and refined language.

H₂0, INDA

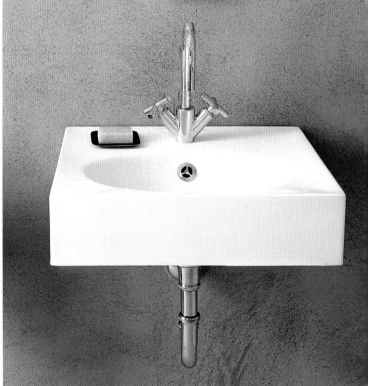

H₂0, INDA

H₂0, INDA

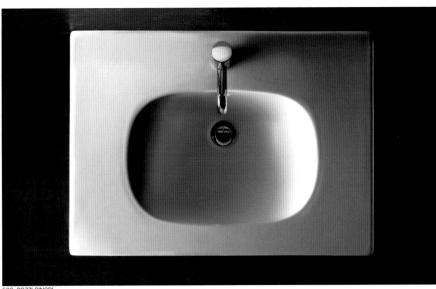

500, POZZI GINORI

JOIN, POZZI GINORI

500, POZZI GINORI

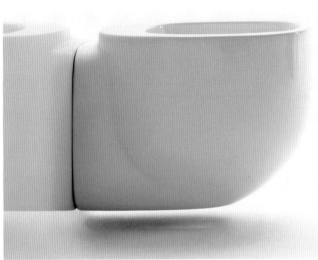

500, POZZI GINORI

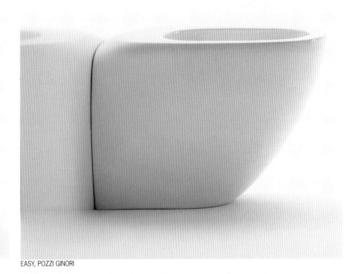

EASY, POZZI GINORI

Q³, POZZI GINORI

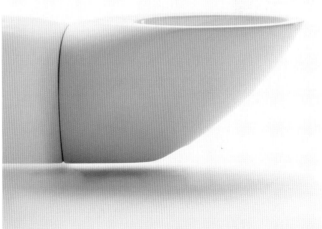

JOIN, POZZI GINORI

04

2000–03. the "design of spaces"

The opening of the new studio in the multistory building on Via Cerva, in 2000, constituted both a symbolic and a practical point of arrival. In 1999 Citterio set up Antonio Citterio and Partners with Patricia Viel; in 2000 he opened a branch in Hamburg, again with Patricia Viel and with Jan Hinrichs; at this point around forty people were working with the architects. In the area of industrial design, the role once played by Glen Oliver Löw was now taken by Toan Nguyen. So the studio had a new dimension in terms of its scale and organization, and one that is not very common in Italy. Comparable with that of similar professional studios abroad, it was a response to the growing numbers of commissions in the field of architecture and design.

Between 1999 and 2002 Citterio had a significant teaching experience at the Academy of Architecture of the University of Italian Switzerland in Mendrisio. As far as architecture is concerned, Citterio and Partners have carried out some important projects in recent years, including the head office of the Edel Company on the Elba River in Hamburg (2002), the Bernd Kortum office building at Neuerwall (2001–02), the Alberto Aspesi offices and textile manufacturing plant at Legnano (2000–01), and the headquarters of the B&B Italia Research and Development Center at Noverate (2000–02). Also underway are the renovation of Linea 1 of the Milan Subway and the concept and design of the Bulgari Hotels and Resorts chain, with luxury accommodation in Milan and Bali. In addition, the Citterio studio has been invited to take part in the competition for the transformation of the historic trade fair district in Milan into a new urban center.

Work has also continued on the fitting out of sales outlets and some prestigious names have been added to the companies that have been collaborating with the architect for some time. They include the stylists Ermenegildo Zegna, Valentino, the Stefanel clothing stores and the De Beers diamond company.

Designing concept stores has become one of the studio's principal activities over time, through reproducible schemes capable of meeting precise needs but which can also be adapted to different situations.

The Antonio Citterio and Partners studio, Via Cerva, Milan, 2000. Design by Antonio Citterio and Patricia Viel.

In industrial design, Citterio now works for a large number of companies, and his products cover practically every type of furnishing for the home or the workplace, from the living area to the office and from the kitchen to the bathroom. These objects configure a sort of ideal, integral and integrated "architect's house," unified by a common sensibility, by a coherent idea of living. The dimension of the individual product, after evolving into that of the system, has been further developed in the direction of a sort of "design of spaces." The preparation of single elements, product of a global planning, answers to the needs of the industrialization of manufacturing processes, but also to those of installation. Spaces and even modes of living and working have changed profoundly, making it necessary to rethink the design of furniture, to turn the objects into adaptable tools that permit variable configurations in space and time and that can be produced, organized and fitted in ways that are prearranged and yet flexible.

The present direction of Citterio's research into industrial design fits into the strategy adopted by companies working in this field, that of a comprehensive planning of modes of operation from the viewpoint of production, communication, distribution and marketing. Citterio is entrusted with the dual task of developing the company's approach to design and helping to implement its business strategy, identifying a possible new type of relationship of which the architect has appeared to

be the most correct interpreter in these years. All this has taken place in close relationship with the further refinement and construction of his own course of development. "I design a great deal," explains Citterio, "although almost exclusively buildings and objects. My practice of architecture is closely tied to direct, hands-on experience; I approach design the same way, looking at the solutions, the details." And he goes on: "Everything has become much more complicated today; my commitments have grown, there are more demands on my time, and it is difficult to find moments for concentration. Increasingly often they come when I'm moving around, on journeys, which have turned into opportunities for thinking and coming up with ideas." It is fairly easy to make out similar themes and experiments and transfers of overall and partial solutions in the projects he has carried out for different companies: elements that cut across the different industries, the result of a global work on design.

Citterio has marked out his own path over time with determination, ability and quality of design. The impression created by his personality, his words and his activity, always undergoing transformation for a variety of reasons, is of a work in progress, not a final achievement but a moment of transition. The research that has taken him in a personal direction, and at the same time allowed him to interpret the needs of his own time, continues.

Ad One system of office furniture, Vitra, 2003.

Edel Music headquarters, Hamburg, Germany, 2002.

Neuerwall office building, Hamburg, Germany, 2001–02.

B&B Italia Research and Development Center, Novedrate, 2002.

Hotel Bulgari, Milan, 2004.

B&B Italia store, Via Durini, Milan, 2002.

B&B Italia showroom, London, 2001.

**Concept of interiors
for an "advanced sports car"**
Alfa Romeo
with Toan Nguyen

Contacted along with other architects as part of a project coordinated by Gino Finizio for the Fiat Style Center, Citterio has had the opportunity to explore the possibilities of an "advanced sports car," and the design of the vehicle's interiors in particular. "The problems that the world of the automobile has to face are certainly enormous and complicated," says the architect. "More in general, they concern the questions of environmental compatibility, of clean energy, and go beyond the contribution that can be made by the individual designer. They involve the whole system of production, the political will to steer our planet and our economy toward a sustainable development. Obviously the Fiat research laboratory has taken a more limited approach, speculating about the characteristics of the sports car, for a make like Alfa Romeo for instance. Speed can no longer be the main factor, and attention is increasingly going to be focused on comfort and the quest for an elegance of style in the overall design of the automobile. I believe that there is a great deal of work to be done on the interiors in particular, which are frequently characterized today by an excess of opulence and ostentation, sometimes verging on kitsch in the use and combination of materials." The concept of an "advanced sports car" for Alfa started out from the idea of a vehicle in which everything disappears from view when it comes to a stop. "The idea is derived from the internal spaces of boats, where everything can be stowed away," he adds. "In this way all that can be recognized is the design of the lines, clean and essential. Then I tried to put the skills I have honed in the design of chairs to work on the design of the seats, reducing the supporting structure and keeping the bulk to a minimum. I studied ways of obtaining a correct and ergonomic seat capable of adapting to variations in people's height and posture in an uncomplicated manner, without forgetting the need to control the microclimate, partly achieved through the use of fabrics that breathe. Finally I decided that the seat had to revolve to permit easy access to the vehicle." The interiors of the automobile look simple and easily worked out. In fact they conceal cunning measures of design capable of providing coherent and natural solutions to complex questions.

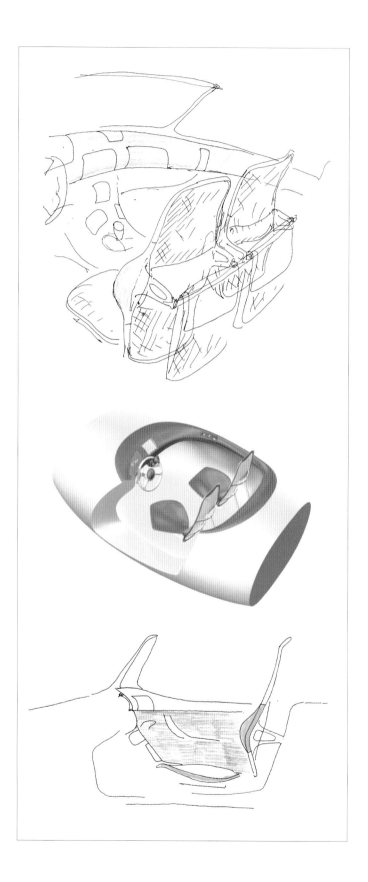

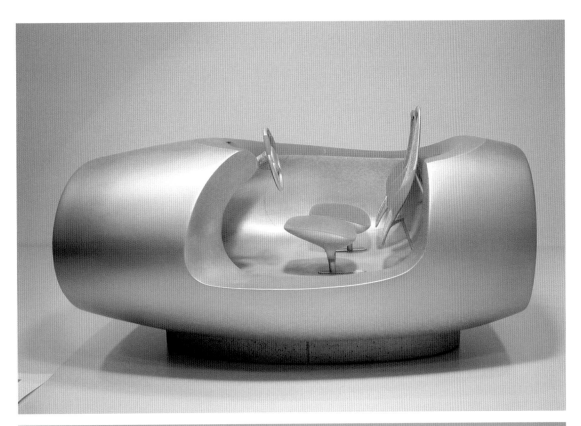

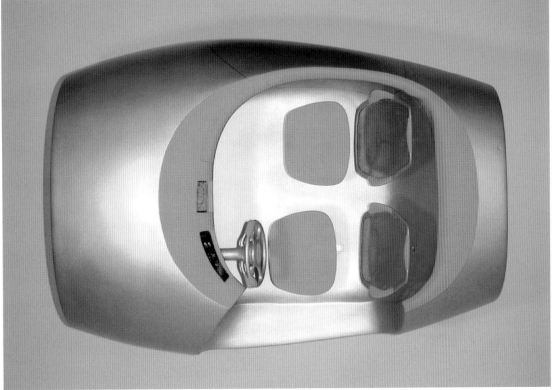

luta seats
B&B Italia

The luta chair and armchair draw on the studies carried out for Web (1998), a chair with a steel structure and seat and back in wire mesh. luta adopts the same structural solutions (in particular the mesh frame), applying them to a wider range of solutions, and above all using a language that has been fully worked out.

The series is made up of two seats, with or without arms, supported by a structure of chrome-plated tubing mounted on a revolving base with four spokes made of die-cast aluminum, or on a slender metal framework in which the legs intersect under the seat. The seat itself is made of plastic or padded and upholstered.

The influence of the models of Charles and Ray Eames is evident, but Citterio has totally revised the object from the viewpoint of the materials and finishes. An original solution, for example, is the seat with arms, where the choice of the wire-mesh frame with metal borders is exploited to generate the gentle curves of the back and arm.

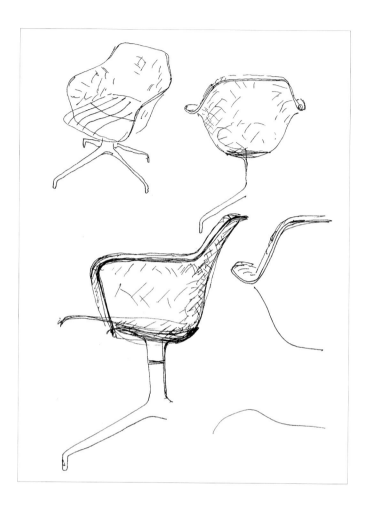

H-Beam and U-Beam lighting systems
Flos
with Glen Oliver Löw

The starting point for the design of the Riga and Beam system of technical lamps was not so much research into the form, which is geometric and essential, but the need to control the characteristics of the light emitted. "I felt it necessary to design a range of large lamps," declares Citterio, "capable of dealing with the specific weight of architecture, of harmonizing with it and becoming a permanent part of it." He went on to develop the idea of architectural space as an integral part of lamp design with Riga and Beam, and in a different way with the Lastra series, also produced by Flos. These are all hanging lamps that require a precise location in space, whether set above a dining table or a work surface. The lamps in the Beam series are defined by a casing of extruded aluminum, painted matt gray or white. The technology for the production of the aluminum permits considerable flexibility in the range on offer, variable in relation to the length of the light sources. The series also has a system for intelligent control of the light, with a program that adjusts the positions of reflectors and prismatic diffusers: the result is an optimal distribution of the light, whether localized or diffused. To meet different lighting requirements two versions of Beam have been designed, with names derived from the H- and U-shaped sections of the lamp's casing. The H-Beam emits light above as well as below, while the U-Beam only projects it upward. This last solution, which also filters the light through lens-shaped prismatic screens designed to control the emission, is particularly effective in workplaces where monitors are used. There is also a Smart Sensor Autodimming version, equipped with a photosensitive cell that is able to adjust the radiant flux in relation to other sources in order to keep the preset level constant. Thus research into optimal standards of illumination has been married with cutting-edge technological solutions to determine not just the quantity but also the quality of the light, through systems of measurement, dosage and compensation. The geometry, cleanliness and essentiality of the design of the wide aluminum bars confers an image on the lamps of the Beam system that is at once high-tech and reassuringly domestic, offering full control as well as naturalness in the way we light our work and living spaces.

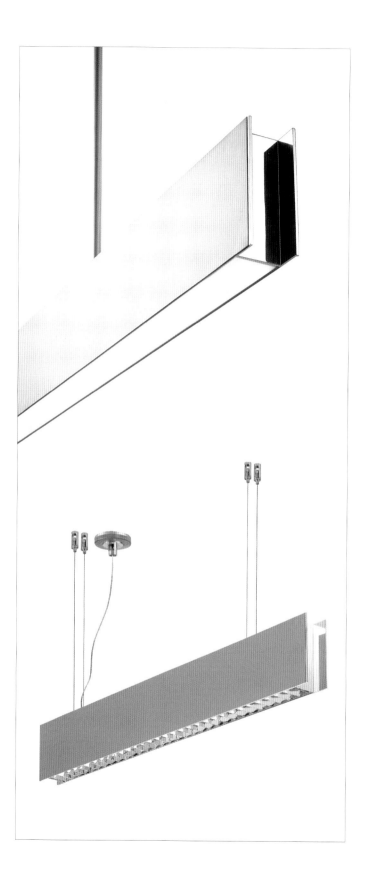

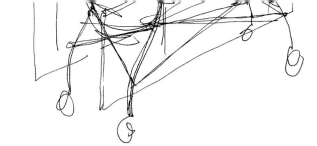

The "minimal" tops made of white polyester or laminate in various shapes and sizes are mounted on a slender metal structure formed of four, slightly curved legs, linked together by thin intersecting rods. The interest of the design lies in its apparent effortlessness, both in the realization of a product which is simplified in its structure and yet couched in a suitable language, and in the equally direct response to the problem of reducing the volume.

It is an object that stems from a thorough familiarity with a number of models of reference, linked to the characteristics of the top rather than to the "scaffolding" of the supporting structure (originally also conceived for the Dolly folding chairs), reinterpreted in a personal way. "My work has numerous references and models," Citterio explains, "yet I always try to understand their distinctive traits fully and, if possible, improve their characteristics. An anonymous object like a hammer is the result of endless improvements made over the course of time; why is it not possible to imagine something similar for the products of design as well?"

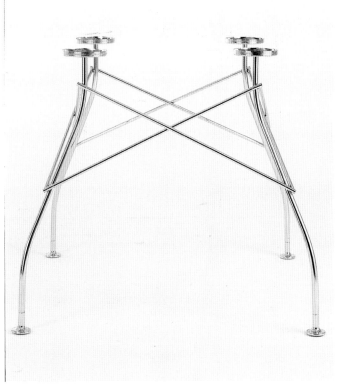

System of office furniture, Vitra

2002, Mobile Elements, with Toan Nguyen;
2003, Ad One, with Toan Nguyen

In the ambit of the research into workplaces Citterio has carried out for Vitra, Mobile Elements represents a different approach to the theme. The main element of the system is the flexible way it allows the furniture to be arranged in spaces, not necessarily just those of the office, but in the home or service areas as well. Certainly not a new question, but one that in this case is tackled in a language which is essential in the materials employed and the solutions provided. The tables, trolleys and storage units are all set on wheels so that they can be moved around. They are visually and physically light since they are supported by a slender structure of slightly bent metal tubing and underlined respectively by rounded tops of white laminate for the tables and shelves of transparent plastic for the trolleys. A few basic elements, such as the legs of the tables or the plastic shelves, can be adapted to construct different elements. The system is completed by a supple dividing element consisting of a metal frame covered with colored elastic fabric, of pleasant and powerful visual impact.

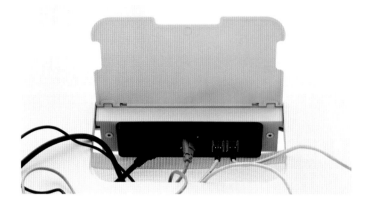

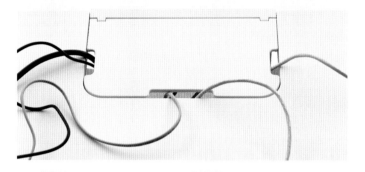

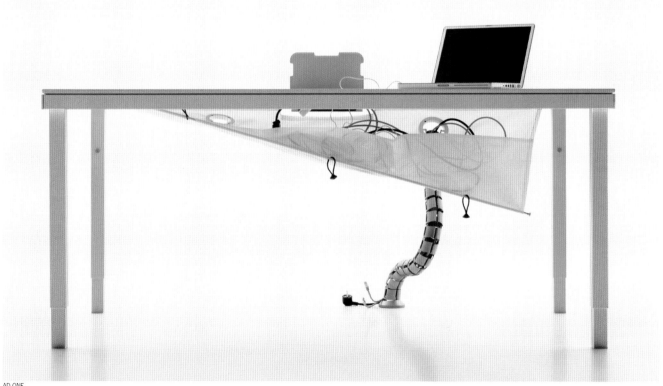

AD ONE

AD ONE

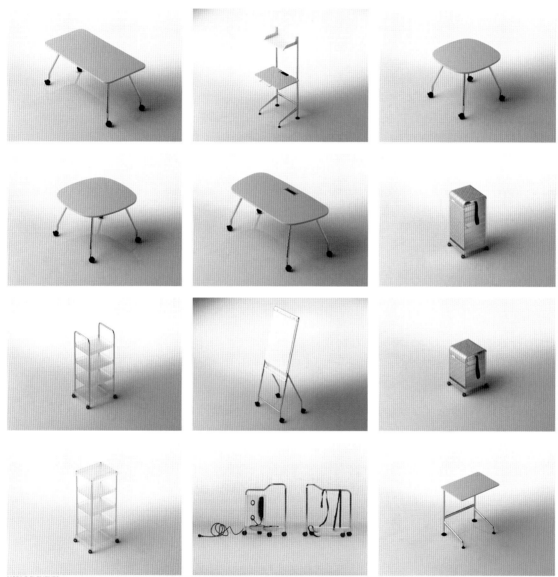

MOBILE ELEMENTS

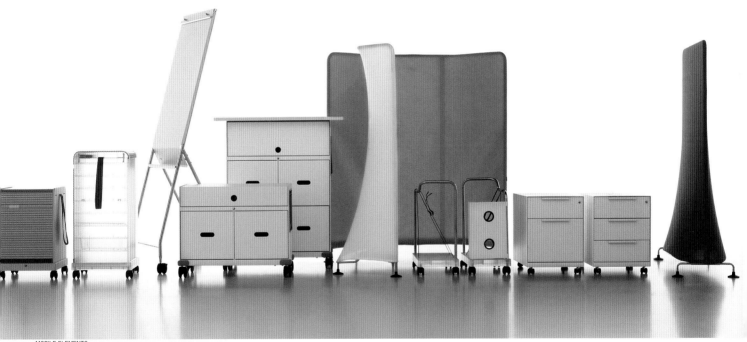

MOBILE ELEMENTS

Axor Citterio range of faucets and sinks
Hansgrohe
with Toan Nguyen

It all started with a faucet, which then led to the design of a complete system of fittings for the bathroom: no longer a separate and isolated room but transparent and open, the space holds a dialogue with the rest of the house. In fact the Axor Citterio line had its origin in the design of elements for the supply of water, but was immediately expanded to embrace a series of sanitary appliances that were stylistically and structurally congruent. The outcome was a specific mode of organizing and locating the elements in relation to different spatial configurations, which could also be determined a priori. Consistent with his "architectural" vision of the relationship between spaces and objects, Citterio has attempted to go beyond the traditional concept of the design of sanitary ware to reflect on its rational positioning in rooms.

The faucet has a geometric and angular design, harking back to a style of the thirties. The handles are in the form of a cross or a lever, distinctive and yet easy to use. The usual circular profile has been replaced by a flat one with sharp edges, giving it an elegant and clean appearance. The same precise style characterizes the sanitary appliances, only slightly rounded on the edges, so that they have a strong visual and spatial impact.

The system as a whole is interesting for its ability to impress a unitary language on the various products and to suggest specific ways of arranging them in space, providing a plan for their physical location.

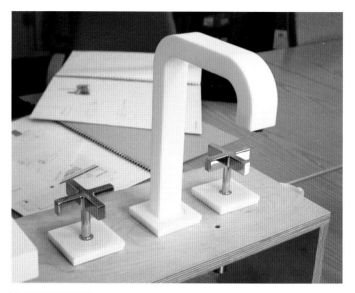

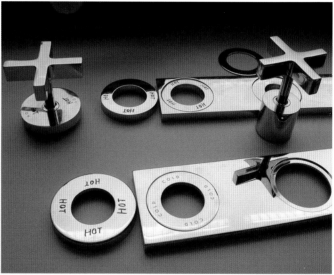

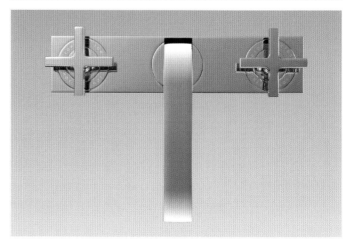

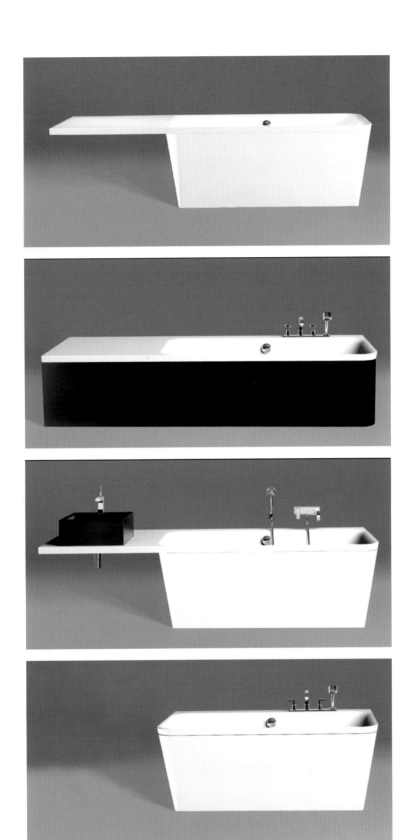

Marcel system of sofas
B&B Italia

The Marcel system of sofas has been created by fusing two stylistically different elements: the reassuring padded structure, set on the floor and given a continuous configuration of seat and back, and the metal frame that runs along the base of the seats, rising to become the support for the cushions. It is a system of deep seats combined with island elements, with adjustable arms and back for a comfortable posture. The back, covered with cushions of various sizes, can in fact be set in different positions: upright for a formal seat and tilted for a more relaxed one. It is interesting to see how Citterio has worked on the modularity of the individual elements, chaise-longue, end piece and ottoman, which can be combined in various ways to create different functional and spatial solutions.

The use of curved metal tubing recalls the research carried out for the Flexform products, but in this case has a largely formal connotation in open contrast with the massive and at the same time functionally efficient structure. Thus it is an arrangement set on the floor which experiments with a different configuration from that of earlier models like Harry and Charles, and one that offers practical and comfortable solutions, such as the adjustable back or the tube running around the edge which becomes an element of support, just like in Freetime.

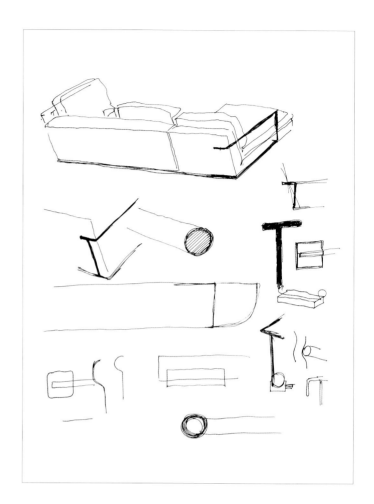

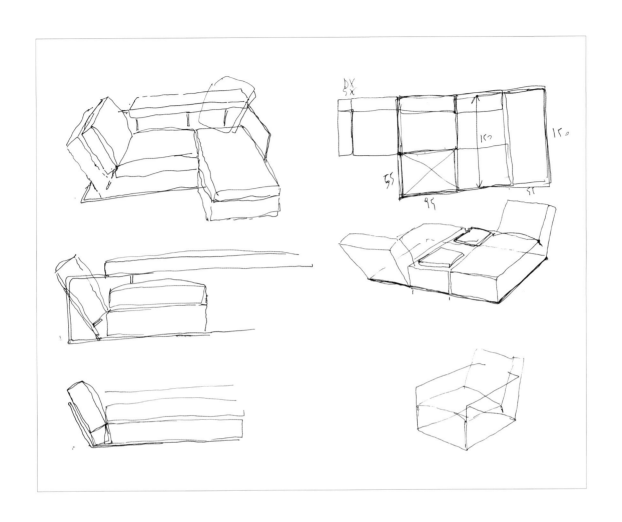

Spoon stool
Kartell
with Toan Nguyen

"The best way to look at Spoon is from behind," points out Citterio, "because it shows the research carried out into the reduction of thicknesses, and above all the intention to break the continuity of tube and seat, which is found in the majority of models in production."

The typology of the bar stool has not often been explored by designers: few such products have achieved great success and visibility.

The aim of Spoon, whose name derives from its sinuous and slender form, was to take a new approach to this kind of object. The innovation lies in the connection of the seat to the central shaft, achieved with an elastic curve of the plastic material (batch-dyed polypropylene) designed to resist the stresses and strains of the load and to offer, at the same time, comfort, stability and flexibility. In addition, the handle that controls the mechanism of the gas pump is set inside the shaft of anodized aluminum. This allows the stool to be raised and lowered but preserves the clean lines of the overall design.

This object of "organic" shape, accentuated by the solution of the four legs, is an imposing presence, especially when lined up at a bar.

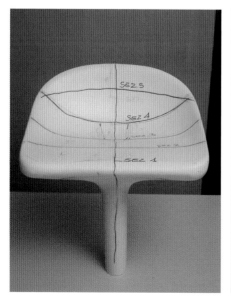
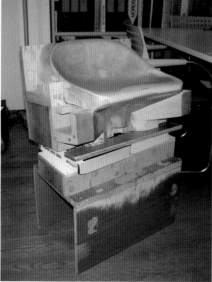

Kelvin lamp
Flos
with Toan Nguyen

The series of table lamps—but a floor version is also envisaged—is the culmination of a program of research into illumination of the table and the workspace, of which Kelvin T Adjustable constitutes the most significant result. There are two archetypal designs for adjustable lamps that have had a long and successful life: Edouard Wilfrid Buquet's counterpoise lamp (1927) and the models with flexible arms, George Carwardine's Anglepoise (1934) and Jacob Jacobsen's Luxo (1937). To move and balance the lamp in space, the former used a rocker arm, the latter a system of springs. Along these same lines we find two classic designs ("what makes an object a classic," says Citterio, "is numbers, its circulation"): Richard Sapper's Tizio (1972) and Michele De Lucchi and Giancarlo Fassina's Tolomeo (1986). With Kelvin Citterio has gone down the road of the spring system but has constructed its form in a more essential manner than the models cited. The starting point for the design was the idea of the clamp that characterizes the base, alluding explicitly to the image of a technical object, of engineering origin and inspired by the construction of bridges rather than tensile structures. The technical and functional solutions linked to the control of the lamp's kinematic mechanism, from the possibility of adjusting it by gentle and steady movements to that of fixing it in a particular position, required careful study. However, the structural details, such as springs and clamps, are deliberately left open to view, in order to convey at once the idea of technology and of attention to modes of production. The result is an object of "polished" design, yet rendered domestic and familiar by the adoption of an external wire, the choice of aluminum as structural material and above all the treatment of the surface of the diffuser. This last consists of a double cap of aluminum and polycarbonate —reminiscent in its profile of a historic model by Arne Jacobsen—with corrugations on its surface that vary in size and depth, following the different inclinations of the truncated cone. The double canopy also prevents excessive heating of the surfaces. In Kelvin the author's language, evident in the overall construction as well as in the handling of details, fits in well with the response to specific requirements of lighting.

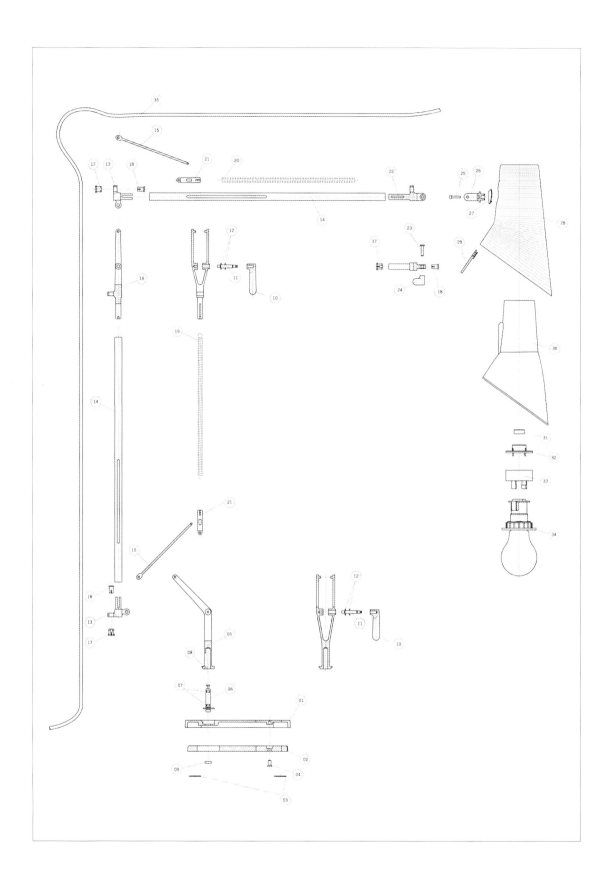

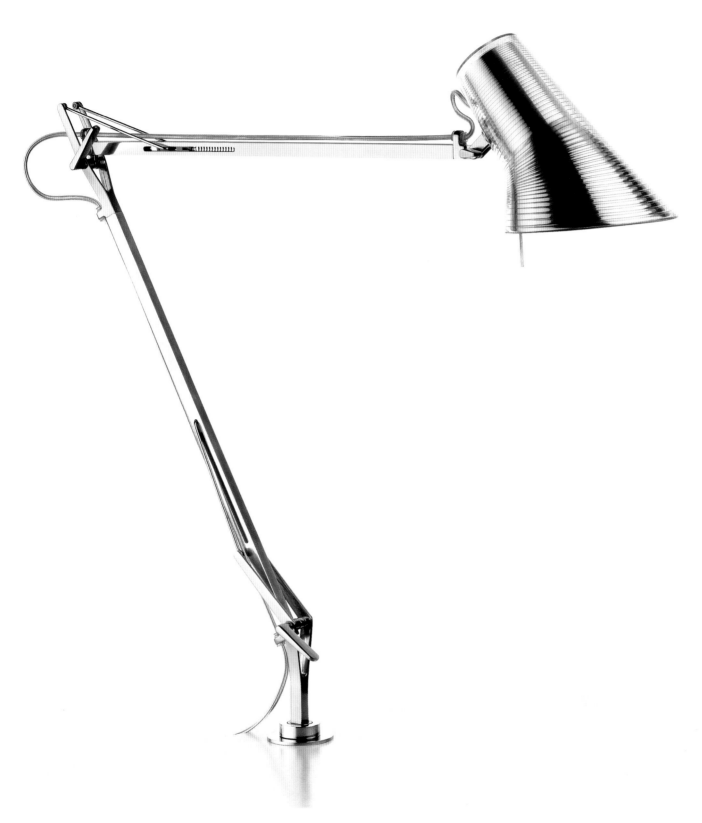

appendices

List of works

1970

Poppy armchair
4P
Antonio Citterio and Paolo Nava

Splaf armchair
Vibieffe
Antonio Citterio, Giandomenico Lodolo
and Paolo Nava

1973

Modulo 30 seating system
B&B Italia
Antonio Citterio and Paolo Nava

1975

ballpoint pen (not produced)
Artvis
Antonio Citterio and Paolo Nava

Baia sofa
B&B Italia
Antonio Citterio and Paolo Nava

1979

Aria and Pasodoble sofa and armchair
Flexform
Antonio Citterio and Paolo Nava

Diesis sofas and armchairs
B&B Italia
Antonio Citterio and Paolo Nava

1980

Divani di Famiglia sofas and armchairs
(Doralice and Filiberto)
Flexform
Antonio Citterio and Paolo Nava

Factory kitchens
Boffi
Antonio Citterio and Paolo Nava

Ialea chair
B&B Italia

Karan d'Ache storage units
Malobbia
Antonio Citterio and Paolo Nava

1981

Eridiana chairs
Xilitalia

Quadrante range of furniture
Xilitalia-B&B Italia
Antonio Citterio and Paolo Nava

1982

Magister sofa
Flexform
Antonio Citterio and Paolo Nava

Ottomana sofa
B&B Italia

1983

Max and Phil sofas
Flexform
with Myriam Veronesi

Milano coffee and tea service
Anthologie Quartett

1984

Metropolis wall container
Tisettanta

1985

Divani di Famiglia sofas and armchairs
(Nonnamaria)
Flexform

Ginger sofa and chaise-longue
Flexform

1986

Sity system of sofas
B&B Italia

1988

Enea wall lamp
Artemide

Italia kitchen
Arclinea

Novecento armchairs
Moroso

1989

Baisity chairs and armchairs
B&B Italia

Domus system of fitted walls
B&B Italia

Draft Line drawing boards
and work tables
Bieffe
with Sergio Brioschi, Glen Oliver Löw

Rich armchairs
Moroso

1990

AC 1, AC 2 and AC 3 adjustable chairs
Vitra

Area seating system for public spaces
Vitra

Cargo system of fittings for stores
Vitrashop-Visplay

1991

AC Novantuno door handles
Fusital

Battista, Filippo, Gastone and Leopoldo
trolleys and tables
Kartell
with Glen Oliver Löw

Oxo computer trolley
Kartell
with Glen Oliver Löw

1992

Axion and Visavis office chairs
Vitra
with Glen Oliver Löw

Balillo sofa and armchair
B&B Italia

Emme system of hospital furniture
Industrie Guido Malvestio
with Stefano Gallizioli

Ephesos office furniture
Olivetti Synthesis
with Sergio Brioschi

Mediterranea kitchen
Arclinea

Spatio system of office furniture
Vitra
with Glen Oliver Löw

Visaroll office chair
Vitra

1993

AC Novantatre door handles
Fusital

Compagnia delle Filippine armchairs
and seats
B&B Italia

Cubis sofas and armchairs
B&B Italia

Cupola hanging lamp
Ansorg
with Glen Oliver Löw

Elettra lighting system
Ansorg
with Glen Oliver Löw

Panama chairs and armchairs
B&B Italia

1994

Ad Hoc system of office furniture
Vitra
with Glen Oliver Löw

Balletto and Canaletto beds
B&B Italia

Foco fireplace
Edilkamin

Mobil storage units
Kartell
with Glen Oliver Löw

Quadra lighting system
Ansorg/Belux
with Glen Oliver Löw

T-Chair office chair
Vitra
with Glen Oliver Löw

Tris tables
Kartell
with Glen Oliver Löw

1995

AC1 Novantacinque and AC2
Novantacinque door handles
Fusital

Florence chairs and armchairs
B&B Italia

Ginger kitchen
Arclinea

Harry system of sofas
B&B Italia

1996

AC Novantacinque door handles
Fusital

Angiolo tables
B&B Italia

Apta collection of furniture
Maxalto-B&B Italia

Artusi, Florida and Florida Young
kitchens
Arclinea

Axess and Quattro office chairs
Vitra
with Glen Oliver Löw

Camera lighting system
Ansorg
with Glen Oliver Löw

Carlotta system of furniture
Flexform

Dolly chair
Kartell
with Glen Oliver Löw

Domusnova system of fitted walls
B&B Italia

Duo lighting system
Ansorg/Belux
with Glen Oliver Löw

Malacorte sofa
B&B Italia

Melandra chairs and armchairs
B&B Italia

Minni chair
Halifax-Tisettanta

Monowall system of office furniture
Vitra
with Glen Oliver Löw

Flatware
Sawaya&Moroni/Guzzini

XL (extra large) system of closets
Tisettanta

1997

Artist computer
Max Data
with Glen Oliver Löw

Basiko sofas
B&B Italia

Dandy armchairs
B&B Italia

1998

ABC system of seats
Flexform

Ad Usum system of office tables
Vitra
with Glen Oliver Löw

Alumina lighting system
Ansorg
with Glen Oliver Löw

Brenda armchair
Flexform

Charles system of sofas
B&B Italia

Citterio 98 flatware
Hackman-Iittala
with Glen Oliver Löw

Lastra hanging lamp
Flos
with Glen Oliver Löw

Pavilion system of doors
Tre Più

Riga wall lamp
Flos
with Glen Oliver Löw

Sumo system of office furniture
Herman Miller

T60 tables
B&B Italia

Theo tables
Flexform

Visasoft office chair
Vitra

Web chair and armchair
B&B Italia

1999

concept and research for television sets
(not produced)
Brionvega
with Toan Nguyen

Centopercento system of storage units
Tisettanta

Cross system of storage units
B&B Italia

Freetime system of sofas
B&B Italia

H_2O bathroom fittings
Inda
with Sergio Brioschi

Kado and Pick Up fittings for stores
Vitrashop-Visplay
with Glen Oliver Löw

Planus system of doors
Tre Più

Solo system of seats
B&B Italia

Storage Wall storage units
Vitra

2000

500 and Join sanitary appliances
Pozzi Ginori
with Sergio Brioschi

concept of interiors for an
"advanced sports car"
(not produced)
Alfa Romeo
with Toan Nguyen

Citterio 2000 flatware
Hackman-Iittala
with Glen Oliver Löw

Citterio Collective Tools 2000
Flatware and utensils
Hackman-Iittala
with Glen Oliver Löw

Dado sofas and armchairs
B&B Italia

Iuta seats
B&B Italia

K2 and Atos door handles
Fusital

Pavilion Light system of doors
Tre Più

Planus system of doors
Tre Più

Simplice Collection range of furniture
Maxalto

Tight chairs and armchairs
B&B Italia

U-Beam and H-Beam lighting systems
Flos
with Glen Oliver Löw

Vademecum systems of office furniture
Vitra
with Glen Oliver Löw

2001

Ad Wall system of office furniture
Vitra

Citterio Collection street furniture
JCDecaux

Domus'00 system of fitted walls
B&B Italia

George system of seats
B&B Italia

Glossy table
Kartell
with Glen Oliver Löw

Groundpiece system of sofas
Flexform

H_2O Frame bathroom fittings
Inda
with Sergio Brioschi

Metropolitan floor and table lamp
Flos

Neolux and XXL floor lamps
Flos

Transphere system of office storage
units
Vitra

2002

Brick lighting system
Ansorg
with Glen Oliver Löw

Convivium kitchen
Arclinea

Door system of closets
B&B Italia

Ground Zero table
Riva 1920

Lightpiece system of seats
Flexform

Mobile Elements system
of office furniture
Vitra
with Toan Nguyen

Oson C, Oson S and Oson CE office
chairs
Vitra

Pavilion Frame system of doors
Tre Più

Plaza ceiling lamp
Flos

ToniX office chairs
Vitra
with Toan Nguyen

U Connect Beam lighting system
Flos

Visacom, Visalounge, Visofa and
Vistable systems of seats and tables
Vitra

2003

AC3 door handles
Fusital
with Toan Nguyen

AC Collection range of furniture
Maxalto-B&B Italia

Ad One system of office furniture
Vitra
with Toan Nguyen

Ad Wing partition
Vitra
with Toan Nguyen

Axor Citterio range of faucets and sinks
Hansgrohe
with Toan Nguyen

Beam F floor lamp
Flos

CEO system of office furniture
Vitra
with Toan Nguyen

Door system of closets
B&B Italia

Easy and Q^3 sanitary appliances
Pozzi Ginori
with Sergio Brioschi

Eileen tables
B&B Italia

Hal floor lamp
Artemide

Kelvin lamp
Flos
with Toan Nguyen

Kidd tables
Flexform

Luxlust, XXL, L and MS lighting systems
Flos

Marcel system of sofas
B&B Italia

Mart armchairs
B&B Italia

Mon Bijou street furniture
Wall
with Toan Nguyen

Ontherocks wall lamp
Flos
with Toan Nguyen

Spoon stool
Kartell
with Toan Nguyen

Te 300 table
B&B Italia

Vic tables
Flexform

Wilson armchair
Flexform

Bibliography

Books

1980

Isa Vercelloni, *1970–1980. Dal design al post design*, Condè Nast, Milan 1980.

1982

Mario Mastropietro, Rolando Gorla (eds.), *Un'industria per il design. La ricerca, i designers, l'immagine B&B Italia*, Lybra Immagine, Milan 1982.

1983

ADI, *Dal cucchiaio alla città nell'itinerario di 100 designer*, Electa, Milan 1983, pp. 56–57.

1984

Andrea Branzi, *La casa calda. Esperienze del Nuovo Design Italiano*, Idea Books, Milan 1984.

1985

Giuliana Gramigna, *1950/1980 Repertorio. Immagini e contributi per una storia dell'arredo italiano*, Arnoldo Mondadori Editore, Milan 1985.

1987

Denis Santachiara, *I segni dell'habitat. Tecnologie e design d'Italia*, ICE, Rome 1987, pp. 26–27.

Fumio Shimizu, Matteo Thun, *Descendants of Leonardo da Vinci. The italian design*, Graphic SHA Publishing, Tokyo 1987.

1988

Giampiero Bosoni, Fabrizio G. Confalonieri, *Paesaggio del design italiano 1972–1988*, Edizioni di Comunità, Milan 1988, pp. 54–55.

Juli Capella, Quimm Larrea, *Architekten, Designer der achtziger-jahre*, Verlag Gerd Hatje, Stuttgart 1988.

Silvio San Pietro, Matteo Vercelloni, *Nuovi negozi a Milano*, L'Archivolto, Milan 1988.

Ugo Volli, *Contro la moda*, Feltrinelli, Milan 1988.

1989

Enzo Frateili, *Continuità e trasformazione. Una storia del disegno industriale italiano 1928/1988*, Alberto Greco, Milan 1989.

1990

Anty Pansera, *Il design del mobile italiano dal 1946 ad oggi*, Laterza, Rome-Bari 1990.

Ezio Manzini, *Artefatti. Verso una nuova ecologia dell'ambiente artificiale*, Domus Academy, Milan 1990.

1991

Franco Zagari, *Sull'abitare. Figura Materialità Densità*, Over, Milan 1991.

Enrico Castelnuovo, Jean Gubler, Dario Matteoni, *L'oggetto misterioso*, in Enrico Castelnuovo (ed.), *Storia del disegno industriale. 1919–1990 Il dominio del design*, vol. III, Electa, Milan 1991.

Maurizio Barberis (ed.), *Le superfici del design*, Idea Books-Progetto DIR, Milan 1991.

1992

Andrée Putman, *The International Design Yearbook 1992*, Calmann & King, London 1992.

Maria Cristina Tommasini, Mario Pancera, *Il design italiano. Protagonisti opere scuole*, Giorgio Mondadori, Milan 1992.

Miriam Veronesi, *Objets et projets. Œuvres de production et œuvres de recerche de createurs du design italien*, ICE, Paris 1992, pp. 36–37.

Antonio D'Auria, Renato De Fusco, *Il progetto del design*, Etaslibri, Milan 1992, p. 81.

1993

Pippo Ciorra, Brigitte Fitoussi, Vanni Pasca, *Antonio Citterio & Terry Dwan architecture & design 1992–1979*, Artemis, Zurich 1993.

Brigitte Fitoussi, *Objects affectifs. Le nouveau design de la table*, Hazan, Paris 1993.

Anty Pansera, *Storia del disegno industriale italiano*, Laterza, Rome-Bari 1993.

Silvio San Pietro, Marco Casamonti, *Nuove abitazioni in Italia*, L'Archivolto, Milan 1993.

1994

Ron Arad, *The International Design Yearbook 1994*, Calmann & King, London 1994.

Vittorio Gregotti, *Le scarpe di Van Gogh. Modificazioni nell'architettura*, Einaudi, Turin 1994, p. 37.

Egidio Mucci (ed.), *Design 2000*, Franco Angeli, Milan 1994.

1995

Pippo Ciorra, *Antonio Citterio, Terry Dwan: ten years of architecture and design*, Birkhäuser, Basel 1995.

Remo Dorigati, Luca Basso Peressut, Elisabetta Ginelli, *L'architettura del caffè*, Abitare Segesta, Milan 1995.

Roberto Marcatti, *Parola di designer*, Abitare Segesta, Milan 1995.

Anty Pansera (ed.), *Dizionario del design italiano*, Cantini, Florence 1995.

Silvio San Pietro, Paola Gallo, *Nuove ville in Italia*, L'Archivolto, Milan 1995.

Carol Soucek King, *Furniture: architects and designers originals*, PBC International, New York 1995.

AA.VV., *Design: storia e storiografia*, Progetto Leonardo, Bologna 1995.

1996

Andrea Branzi, *Il Design italiano 1964–1990*, Electa, Milan 1996.

Fulvio Carmagnola, Vanni Pasca, *Minimalismo etica delle forme e nuova semplicità del design*, Lupetti, Milan 1996, p. 9.

Stefano Casciani, *The art factory. Italian design: towards the Third Millennium*, Abitare Segesta, Milan 1996.

Laura Lazzaroni, *35 anni di design al Salone del mobile 1961–1996*, Cosmit, Milan 1996.

1997

François Fauconnet, Brigitte Fitoussi, Karin Leopold, *Vitrines d'architecture. Les boutiques à Paris*, Editions du Pavillon de l'Arsenal, Picard, Paris 1997.

Silvio San Pietro, Paola Gallo, *Nuovi negozi in Italia 4*, L'Archivolto, Milan 1997.

Marta Weiss, Tibor Kalman, *Chairman Rolf Fehlbaum*, German Design Council and Lars Müller, Ditzingen 1997.

1998

Omar Calabrese (ed.), *Il modello italiano. Le forme della creatività*, Skira, Milan 1998.

Mario Campi, Pippo Ciorra, *Young Italian Architects*, Birkäuser, Basel 1998.

Richard Sapper, *The International Design Yearbook 1998*, Laurence King Publishing, London 1998.

Lorenzo Soledad, *New european furniture design*, Links International, Barcelona 1998.

Penny Sparke, *A Century of Design*, Reed Books, London 1998.

Umberto Colombo, *Caratteri peculiari del modello produttivo industriale italiano*, in Omar Calabrese (ed.), *Il modello italiano. Le forme della creatività*, Skira, Milan 1998, pp. 3–13.

Giorgio De Michelis, *Aperto, molteplice, continuo*, Dunod, Milan 1998.

1999

Giuliana Gramigna, Paola Biondi, *Il design in Italia dell'arredamento domestico*, Allemandi, Turin 1999, pp. 143–47.

Claudia Neumann, *Design Lexikon Italien*, Dumont, Cologne 1999.

Clino Trini Castelli, *Transitive design. A design language for the Zeroes*, Electa, Milan 1999.

Enrico Morteo, *Antonio Citterio*, in Mario Mastropietro, Renato Gorla (ed.), *Un'industria per il design. La ricerca, i designers, l'immagine B&B Italia*, Lybra Immagine, Milan 1999, p. 264.

Andrea Branzi, *Introduzione al design italiano. Una modernità incompleta*, Baldini&Castoldi, Milan 1999, p. 170.

2000

Michael Erlhoff, Jutta Frings, *4: 3. 50 Jahre italienisches & deutsches Design*, Kunst- und Ausstellunghalle, Bonn 2000, pp. 150–51.

Orietta Fiorenza, Massimo Roj (eds.), *Workspace/Workscape. I nuovi scenari dell'ufficio*, Skira, Milan 2000.

Carol Soucek King (ed.), *Designing with spirituality*, PBC International, New York 2000.

Gianni Malossi, "Design di moda?," in *ADI Design Index 1998–1999*, Editrice Compositori, Bologna 2000, p. 35.

2001

Paola Antonelli, *Worksphere. Design and contemporary work styles*, The Museum of Modern Art, New York 2001.

Andrea Branzi (ed.), *Italia e Giappone: Design come stile di vita in paesaggi italiani*, Nihon Keizai Shimbun, Tokyo 2001, pp. 38–39.

Aldo Colonetti (ed.), *Grafica e design a Milano 1933–2000*, Abitare Segesta, Milan 2001, pp. 181–84, 194–95.

Luigi Settembrini (ed.), *1951–2001 Made in Italy?*, Skira, Milan 2001, pp. 104–16.

Fulvio Carmagnola, *Vezzi insulsi e frammenti di storia universale. Tendenze estetiche nell'economia del simbolico*, Luca Sossella, Rome 2001, p. 62.

Gabriella Lojacono, *Le imprese del sistema arredamento. Strategie di design, prodotto e distribuzione*, Etas, Milan 2001.

Sergio Polano, *Achille Castiglioni, tutte le opere 1938–2000*, Electa, Milan 2001, p. 9.

Maurizio Vitta, *Il progetto della bellezza. Il design fra arte e tecnica, 1851–2001*, Einaudi, Turin 2001, p. 310.

Giuseppe Siri, *La psiche del consumo*, Franco Angeli, Milan 2001.

Giuseppe Maione, *Le merci intelligenti. Miti e realtà del capitalismo contemporaneo*, Bruno Mondadori, Milan 2001.

Enzo Mari, *Progetto e passione*, Bollati Boringhieri, Turin 2001, p. 52.

2002
Giampiero Bosoni (ed.), *La cultura dell'abitare. Il design in Italia 1945–2001*, Skira, Milan 2002.

2003
Stanley Abercrombie, *A century of Interior design 1900–2000. A timetable of the design, the designers, the products and the profession*, Rizzoli New York, New York 2003.

Arian Mostaedi, *Cool Shops*, Links Publishing Group, Barcelona 2003.

Giampaolo Fabris, *Il nuovo consumatore: verso il postmoderno*, Franco Angeli, Milan 2003, p. 49.

Alberto Bassi, *Italian Lighting Design 1945–2000*, Electa, Milan 2003.

Vilém Flusser, *Filosofia del design*, Bruno Mondadori Editore, Milan 2003, p. 5.

Magazines
1980
Daniele Baroni (ed.), "Antonio Citterio e Paolo Nava," in *Interni*, March 1980, n.p.

Roberto Beretta, "Diesis: un esempio di coerenza. Un progetto di Antonio Citterio e Paolo Nava B&B Italia," in *Rassegna*, 57, June 1980, pp. 67–71.

1983
"Salle d'exposition Milan," in *L'architecture d'aujourd'hui*, 230, November 1983, pp. 104–05.

1984
Alessandro Colbertaldo, "Shop Design," in *Interni*, May 1984, pp. 2–5.

1985
Cristina Morozzi, "Ritratto di un designer: in viaggio alla ricerca dei maestri," in *Modo*, 85, December 1985, pp. 30–33.

"Restructuration du Musée de Brera Milan," in *L'architecture d'aujourd'hui*, 240, September 1985, pp. 22–23.

1987
"Il progetto della storia," interview by Joseph Rykwert with Vittorio Magnago Lampugnani, in *Domus*, 683, May 1987.

Manolo De Giorgi, "Antonio Citterio. Afrikahuis ad Amsterdam," in *Domus*, 686, September 1987, pp. 64–73.

1988
Vernon Mays, "Esprit Amsterdam: well-chosen words," in *Progressive Architecture*, September 1988, pp. 66–73.

"Opulenza ma 'scabra ed essenziale,'" in *Abitare*, December 1988, pp. 128–37.

"Strenge Ästhetic: Esprit Mailand. Die Architektur zwingt zur Konzentration," in *Architektur & Wohnen*, February–March 1988, pp. 90–93.

1989
Edie Cohen, "Two by Citterio & Dwan," in *Interior Design*, April 1989, pp. 284–88.

1990
Brigitte Fitoussi, "Antonio Citterio," in *L'architecture d'aujourd'hui*, July 1990, pp. 202–22.

"From the Architect's account. Antonio Citterio & Terry Dwan: casa sperimentale, Kumamoto," in *Domus*, February 1990, pp. 8–9.

Hernàn Grafias, "Antonio Citterio entre la arquitectura y el diseño," in *Diseño*, September–November 1990, pp. 56–61.

Enrico Morteo, "Antonio Citterio per Vitra, AC 1 High Tech," in *Domus*, September 1990, pp. 112–15.

Karen D. Stein, "Shadow Box," in *Architectural Record*, April 1990, pp. 78–83.

Sophie Tasma Anargyros, "Esprit atterrit Place de la Victoires à Paris," in *Intramuros*, March–April 1990, pp. 22–26.

1991
Brigitte Fitoussi, "Virgin Megastore à Milan," in *L'architecture d'aujourd'hui*, December 1991, pp. 150–52.

"Japan: West-Östliches Würfelspiel," in *Häuser*, 5, 1991, pp. 146–51.

José Maria Marzo, "Tienda Esprit," in *Diseño Interior*, May 1991, pp. 82–87.

Pino Scaglione, "Antonio Citterio," in *d'A*, 1991, p. 68.

Deyan Sudjic, "A moving target," in *Blueprint*, September 1991, pp. 30–32.

Sophie Tasma Anargyros, Antonio Citterio, in *Intramuros*, September–October 1991, pp. 38–42.

1992
Brigitte Fitoussi, "Showroom Corrente à Tokyo, Boutique Fausto Santini à Paris," in *L'architecture d'aujourd'hui*, September 1992, pp. 152–55.

Mario Gerosa (ed.), "Antonio Citterio: come Eames, più di Eames," in *Interni*, January–February 1992, pp. 122–28.

Rita Imwinkelried, "Antonio Citterio aus Meda," in *Hoch Parterre*, January 1992, pp. 54–57.

"Il lusso del vuoto," in *Gap Casa*, November 1992, pp. 82–85.

Veronica Pini (ed.), "Il progetto della qualità. Colloquio con Antonio Citterio," in *Interni*, Annual casa, 1992, pp. 58–60.

Dada Sanz y Alvaro Varela, "Showroom de Corrente in Tokyo," in *Diseño Interior*, 11, 1992, pp. 40–43.

"Vom Reiz der Klarheit," in *Ait*, May 1992, pp. 54–66.

Aidan Walker, "The Music Megas," in *Designers' Journal*, January 1992, p. 28.

1993
"Antonio Citterio & Terry Dwan. Fabbrica di imbottiti a Neuenburg," in *Abitare*, September 1993, pp. 182–85.

"Concours pour le mobilier hospitalier," in *Intramuros*, May–June 1993, pp. 38–39.

"Main man in Milan Antonio Citterio," in *Design Week*, 41, October 1993.

Ursula Dietz, "Modern von Renaissance behütet," in *Häuser*, 1, 1993, pp. 30–33.

Eleonora Restelli, "Antonio Citterio: Designer per vocazione," in *Office Furniture*, 62, supplement 1993–94, pp. 14–19.

1994
"Antonio Citterio and Terry Dwan," in *Axis*, summer 1994, pp. 134–37.

Antonella Boisi, "Spazi puri," in *Interni*, November 1994, pp. 82–91.

Stefano Casciani, Antonio Citterio, "Sistema di cassettiere-contenitori," in *Abitare*, April 1994, pp. 194–95.

Cecilia Fabiani, "Light. Die reduzierten Ladenbauten Antonio Citterios," in *Ait*, March 1994, p. 46.

Gino Finizio, "La riduzione del segno," in *Ottagono*, September–November 1994, pp. 82–87.

Vanni Pasca (ed.), "Minimalismo come complessità. Intervista con Antonio Citterio," in *Interni*, Annual casa, 1994, pp. 26–33.

"Tre negozi per Fausto Santini," in *Domus*, September 1994, pp. 60–65.

Federica Zanco, "Una famiglia di lampade," in *Domus*, March 1994, pp. 56–59.

Raimonda Riccini, "'History from things.' Note sulla storia del disegno industriale," in *Archivi e imprese*, 14, December 1994, pp. 231–35.

1995
Antonella Boisi, "Ad Hoc per l'ufficio del Duemila," in *Interni*, May 1995, pp. 134–39.

Antonio Citterio, "L'evoluzione dello spazio cucina," in *Interni*, Annual cucina, 1995, pp. 5–16.

Robert Haidinger, "Antonio Citterio: Möbel mit Logik und System," in *Der Standard*, Album Detail, March 1995, pp. 2–6.

Beverly Pearce, "Process revealed by design," in *Metropolis*, May 1995, p. 64.

Alberto Bassi, "Gli archivi del progetto," in *Archivi e imprese*, 11–12, January–December 1995, pp. 144–60.

1996
"Antonio Citterio. Sull'aria di un progetto coerente," in *Interni*, September 1996, pp. 166–69.

Albrecht Bangert, "Mailand meets New York," in *Elle Décoration*, May–June 1996, pp. 76–81.

Antonella Boisi, "Lo spazio Cerruti," in *Interni*, October 1996, pp. 90–97.

Stefano Casciani, "L'arte nel cuore della luce," in *Abitare*, December 1996, pp. 91–101.

"Come un classico ridisegnato. Citterio per Fusital," in *Ottagono*, September–November 1996, p. 160.

Rudolf Novak, "Doppelpaß," in *Möbel Raum Design*, December–January 1996, pp. 56–61.

Phil Patton, "A Classic goes to Europe, returning Brand new," in *Sunday*, September 8, 1996, p. 49.

Elena Plebani, "Un appartement milanais d'Antonio Citterio," in *Decors*, 992, September–November 1996, p. 172–79.

Klaus Schmidt-Lorenz, "Erfolg durch Gespür," in *Design Report*, January–February 1996, pp. 47–53.

Rosaria Zucconi, "Boutique,"
in *Elle Décor*, September 1996,
pp. 35–36.

1997

"Antonio Citterio pour Cerruti,"
in *Architecture interieure creé*, 275,
1997, pp. 118–19.

Fabrizio Bergamo, "Apta, dal mobile
all'ambiente," in *Interni*, May 1997,
pp. 110–13.

Heike Bering, "Antonio Citterio," in
Möbel Interior Design, December 1997,
pp. 91–95.

"Citterio & Dwan boutique Cerruti
à Milan," in *L'architecture d'aujourd'hui*,
June 1997, pp. 102–03.

Gabriele di Matteo, "Nelle nicchie
del Made in Italy," in *La Repubblica*,
Casa & Design supplement,
April 18, 1997, p. 11.

"Form und Flexibilität," in *Design Report*,
February 1997, pp. 30–33.

Lucas Hollweg, "The design of a serious
man," in *The Independent Review* (The
Independent on Sunday), February 2,
1997, pp. 52–53.

Kicca Menoni, "Antonio & Terry,"
in *Interni*, supplement to *Panorama*,
December 1997, pp. 69–81.

Michelle Ogundhein, "Citterio modern
heroes," in *Elle décoration*, February
1997, pp. 86–88.

Annamaria Scevola, "Declinare
un'immagine," in *Ottagono*,
June–August 1997, pp. 106–09.

Federica Tommasi, "Uno scenario Ad
Hoc," in *Ufficio Stile*, January–February
1997, p. 44.

"Vom neuen poetischen Purismus,"
in *AD*, February–March 1997,
pp. 200–04.

1998

Antonella Boisi, "Tra rigore e poesia,"
in *Interni*, May 1998, pp. 90–97.

"Casa unifamiliare, Cene, Bergamo,"
in *Domus*, February 1998, pp. 28–33.

Stefano Casciani, "Antonio Citterio.
Mode e stili," in *Abitare*, October 1998,
pp. 132–33.

Edie Cohen, "The new domestic
landscape," in *Interior design*, August
1998, pp. 138–43.

Regina Decoppet, Franziska Müller,
"Reduzierte sprache in Arkitektur und
Design," in *Ideales Heim*, June 1998,
pp. 91–96.

Anne Draeger, "Les pros de la déco
chez eux. Antonio Citterio, un designer
chaleureux," in *Madame Figaro*,
March 1998, pp. 76–85.

Daniela Falsitta, "La casa da vivere,"
in *Interni*, January–February 1998,
pp. 132–33.

"Funktionales volumen," in *Möbel
Interior Design*, July 1998, pp. 50–51.

"Un'ipotesi di lavoro. Il progetto
di immagine coordinata della
metropolitana milanese linea 1,"

in *Ottagono*, September–November
1998, pp. 48–51.

"Mariella Burani en Milan," in *Diseño
Interior*, 77, 1998, pp. 86–87.

Enrico Morteo, "La struttura della luce,"
in *Interni*, April 1998, pp. 186–87.

Michelle Ogundehin, "The italian job,"
in *Elle décoration*, December 1998,
pp. 74–81.

Maddalena Padovani, "Una scatola
di luce," in *Panorama*, Interni
supplement , June 5, 1998, pp. 54–59.

"Papillon," in *Ottagono*, June–August
1998, pp. 146–49.

"Profilen Citterio," in *Elle Interiör*,
March 1998, pp. 30–35.

Caroline Roux, "Staying power," in *ID*,
January–February 1998, pp. 68–69.

Carla Shumann, "Privatwelt eines Top-
Designers. Citterio pur," in *Architecture
& Whonen*, August–September 1998,
pp. 38–45.

"Tiendas Fausto Santini," in *Diseño
Interior*, January 1998, pp. 120–23.

"Vivienda Citterio-Dwan," in *Diseño
Interior*, 76, 1998, pp. 36–41.

1999

Evi Mibelli, "Ritorno alle origini,"
in *Interni*, March 1999, pp. 76–81.

2000

Laura Asnaghi, "Citterio, o la semplicità
come etica," in *La Repubblica*, Affari
e finanza insert, November 6, 2000.

Pamela Buxton, "Family ties," in *Design
Week*, 27 October 2000, pp. 16–17.

Antonio Citterio, "Cene Villa Complex,"
in *Zlaty Rez*, 20, 2000, pp. 34–37.

"Antonio Citterio, Cino Zucchi, Philippe
Délis, Vignelli Ass., Pietro Clemente,
Tedesco, Ariatta, Milano: Ansaldo la città
delle culture. Concorso internazionale
di progettazione," in *Abitare*,
supplement, June 2000.

2001

Antonio Citterio, "Villa nel Comense,"
in *Casa D*, April 2001, pp. 58–79.

Edie Cohen, "Studio Central," in *Interior
Design*, May 2001, pp. 328–31.

"La factoria Citterio," in *Diseño interior*,
April 2001, pp. 138–47.

Phoebe Greenwood, "Un tunnel di luce,"
in *Domus*, October 2001, pp. 98–107.

IMade 2001, exhibition catalogue,
Clac, Cantù 2001, pp. 96–99.

Fabrizio Todeschini, "Antonio Citterio,"
in *Habitat ufficio*, March 2001,
pp. 166–73.

2002

Stefano Casciani, "Costruire ad
Amburgo," in *Domus*, November 2002,
pp. 74–87.

Edie Cohen, *"Antonio Citterio,"*
in *Interior Design*, December 2002,
pp. 12–16.

Lauren Goldstein, "Staying in style,"
in *Time*, December 16, 2002, p. 32.

"Highlight," in *Architektur
Innenarchitektur Technischer Ausbau*,
1–2, 2002, pp. 77–85.

Dane McDowell, "Géométrie dans
l'espace Carimate," in *Résidences
décoration*, June 2002, pp. 60–69.

Jan Van Rossem, "Antonio Citterio:
erneuerer der moderne," in *Architektur
& Wohnen*, March 2002, pp. 77–87.

Petra Trefalt, "Zeitloser Modernist,"
in *Design report*, July 2002,
pp. 50–54.

Matteo Vercelloni, "B&B Italia Store:
uno spazio per il design," in *Interni*,
December 2002, pp. 177–91.

Ahrens Von Inge, "Herzstück vom Profi,"
in *Boulevard*, October 2002, p. 8.

Ulla Rogalski, "Ein Moderner geht seinen
Weg," in *Handelszeitung, casa special*,
March 2002, p. 7.

Rosaria Zucconi, "Glamour italiano,"
in *Elle Décor*, September 2002,
pp. 166–77.

2003

Alberto Bassi, "I percorsi di Citterio,"
in *Auto & Design*, 142, October 2003,
pp. 66–69.

Antonella Boisi, "Spazio astratto,"
in *Interni*, April 2003, pp. 242–47.

Stefano Casciani, "L'albergo modello,"
in *Domus hotel extra*, November 2003,
pp. 76–81.

Cornelia Krause, "Zwei Ansichten,"
in *Deutsche Bauzeitung*, 9, 2003,
pp. 63–67.

"Le pape du design," in *Le figaro
magazine*, March 15, 2003, p. 100.

Michele Reboli, "Il campus B&B Italia
a Novedrate," in *Casabella*, 715,
October 2003, pp. 74–91.

Alberto Bassi, "Design e tecnologia.
B&B Italia e la schiumatura di
poliuretano a freddo in stampo,"
in *Casabella*, 715, October 2003,
pp. 74–91.

Frank A. Reinhardt, "Von der Armatur
zum Raum," in *Design report*, 4,
2003, pp. 40–43.

"The rustic man," in *Intra*,
April 2003, pp. 36–38.

Ingrid Sommar, "Fran tunnelbana
till vattenkran," in *Arkitektur*,
September 2003, pp. 62–66.

Aleksandra Stepnikowska, "Design jest
odpowiedzia," in *Architektura murator*,
4, 2003, pp. 74–75.

Paola Tamborini, "Ausgangspunkt Raum
Antonio Citterio," in *Raum und Wohnen*,
3, 2003, pp. 122–28.

Paul Taylor, "Enduring style," in *The New
Zealand Herald*, July 23, 2003, p. 10.

Biography

Antonio Citterio was born in Meda in 1950 and took a degree in architecture at the Milan Polytechnic. In 1972 he opened a studio of his own, focusing initially on industrial design and then, in 1981, turning his attention to architectural and interior design as well. From 1987 to 1996 he was in partnership with Terry Dwan. In 1999, with Patricia Viel, he founded Antonio Citterio and Partners, a studio that works in the fields of architecture, industrial design and graphics.

He collaborates with numerous Italian and foreign companies specializing in products of design, including Ansorg, Arclinea, Axor-Hansgrohe, B&B Italia, Flexform, Flos, Fusital, Guzzini, Hackman-Iittala, Inda, Kartell, Maxalto, Pozzi Ginori-Sanitec Group, Tre Più, Vitra and Wall.

In April 2000 he opened a new studio on Via Cerva 4 in Milan, and the following May one on Wrangelstrasse 75b in Hamburg.

From 1999 to 2002 he taught at the Academy of Architecture of the University of Italian Switzerland in Mendrisio.

He was awarded the Compasso d'Oro-ADI in 1987 and 1995.

Some of his objects are on display in the world's major collections of design, including: Mobil and Battista (Kartell) at the Museum of Modern Art in New York; Mobil, Battista, Dolly, Gastone and Oxo (Kartell) in the permanent collection of the Centre Pompidou, Paris; the Citterio Tools 2000 flatware (Hackman-Iittala) and Axor faucets and fittings (Hansgrohe) in the permanent design collection of the Museum of Architecture and Design in Chicago.

Photo credits

All the illustrations in this volume come from the Antonio Citterio and Partners studio, which has given permission for their publication.

The photographs were taken by, among others:

Ramesh Amruth: p. 95 center and bottom

Aldo Ballo: pp. 10 top, 30 left, 51

Gabriele Basilico: pp. 7, 8 top and center, 29, 30 right, 31 right, 32 bottom, 36, 38 bottom, 40, 41, 42, 44 bottom, 45, 46, 47 bottom, 48, 49, 57, 68, 69, 153

Gert von Bassewitz: p. 50

Fabrizio Bergamo: pp. 20 center and bottom, 26, 27, 67, 122 bottom, 123, 124 bottom, 125, 127, 146, 147, 148, 155 bottom right and left, 158, 170, 171

Santi Caleca: p. 10 bottom

Hans Georg Esch: pp. 105, 106 bottom

Piero Fasanotto: pp. 24, 142, 174, 175, 178, 179

Ramak Fazel: p. 161

Klaus Frahm: p. 155 top

Hans Hansen: pp. 15, 77, 82, 83, 84, 88, 89, 90, 91, 97, 98 top right, bottom, 99, 101, 154, 164, 165

Stefan Kirchner: pp. 61, 62

Massimo Listri (*AD Architectural Digest*): p. 33

Simona Pesarini & Alberto Bulina: p. 53

Pesarini & Michetti: pp. 18, 108, 109, 128, 131, 162, 163, 172 top, 173

Francesco Radino: p. 31 left

Studio Frea: p. 120

Studio IKB Carlo Gessaga and Bruno Vezzoli: pp. 20 top, 140, 141 bottom

Studio On Time: p. 121

Leo Torri: pp. 149, 150, 151, 155 center

Felix Wey: pp. 74, 75

Gionata Xerra: p. 60 right

Miro Zagnoli: pp. 12, 71, 96 top and bottom

Holders of rights to any unattributed photograph sources should contact the publisher.